INBOUND MARKETING BOOK

For Professionals: Proven Three-step
NO BULLSH*T SYSTEM
Generates Quality Inquiries Weekly

TOM POLAND

ISBN: 978-0-9775032-4-7

Free Resources Mentioned in This book

Throughout this book I mention multiple examples of marketing Assets that bring to life the three-part marketing model that I outline in Chapters five, six, and seven. The list of Assets and links below are offered with a view to shining a brighter light on how to implement my recommendations by giving you actual, real-life examples. I've list them all here in one place to save you the time and trouble of searching through the entire book.

All the resources mentioned below are free and **the first three will most likely prove to be the most valuable** to you.

1. Lead Generation Demonstration registration page example: www.LeadGenDemo.com

Make sure that you register for, and attend, my online demonstration via this web page because this is a live version of what I teach in this book. Attending this demonstration will show you in real time how I educate, motivate, and qualify prospects.

2. Consult web page example: www.BookAChatWithTom. com

At the end of many of my online presentations I will offer a Consult. This is the page that I direct interested prospects to, and virtually all of my Consults go via this page first to ensure that my guest and I are likely to have a fit between their needs and budget and what I can provide. I recommend you do that same for your inquiries.

3. Program sales page example: www.iWantSolo.com

In Chapter Seven, I explain when and why you should offer a Consult at the end of your online demonstration and when and why you should offer for people to buy directly from you, bypassing the Consult. This is the sales page I direct attendees to if I am employing the latter option.

4. Other Educational Marketing Assets that generate email subscriber opt-ins

In Chapter Eight, I list several other "Plan B" assets that generate email subscriber opt-ins together with their conversion percentages. These include:

> **A.** Five Hour Challenge: **www.FiveHourChallenge. com**
>
> **B.** Ten minute "evergreen" replay: **www.LeadsInTenMinutes.com**
>
> **C.** Interactive Model: **www.leadsology.guru/the-model/**
>
> **D.** Diagnostic Tool: **www.leadsology.guru/diagnostic/**

5. **Social Media (and other miscellaneous) Assets**

I mention in this book that Social Media is not designed for generating new client inquires, but it still has a big part to play in your marketing because it can keep your "Brand in their Brain until they are ready to Buy." Here are the links to some of my Social Media pages:

A. Facebook Group: **www.facebook.com/groups/leadsology/**

B. LinkedIn Profile: **www.linkedin.com/in/tompoland/**

C. Twitter: **www.twitter.com/tompoland** @tompoland

D. Website: **www.Leadsology.Guru**

E. Podcast: **www.leadsology.guru/podcast/**

F. Blog: **www.leadsology.guru/blog/**

Contents

PREFACE

Who This Book Is For

THIS BOOK IS for professionals who offer advice or a service which involves an ongoing relationship with their clients and for which they charge thousands or tens of thousands per transaction.

That includes, but is not limited to, coaches, trainers, financial planners, SaaS developers, and consultants.

Such marketing requires a specialized method because it's more akin to proposing marriage than it is to selling a washing machine, because marketing such services requires you to establish a very high level of trust prior to suggesting that a prospect considers working with you.

This book lays out the very best way of implementing such a method into your business.

It is not offered as a complete treatment of Inbound Marketing, but rather it presents one specific method that is the most efficient and effective method for generating a consistent weekly flow of high-quality new client inquiries.

Why I wrote this book

I wrote this book so that others who are marketing services or advice might find the journey toward establishing a weekly flow of new client inquiries, much shorter than the one that I endured.

I started the journey toward this book decades ago and with two distinct advantages.

Firstly, I was $80,000 in debt with zero assets and zero income. That meant I had no money to invest in marketing.

Secondly, I was ignorant regarding how to generate *quality, inbound* new client inquiries for my services.

You may think that having no money and no inbound marketing expertise would be a tremendous handicap to achieving my goal of prosperity that would follow once I had established a relentless flow of high-quality, inbound leads.

Regarding having no money to spend on marketing; that apparent disadvantage turned out to be an advantage because I figured out how to generate new clients without cost.

Regarding being ignorant; it's not like I hadn't tried to learn from others. Decades prior, I had literally travelled the world and sat at the feet of marketing masters in workshops and seminars. I would invariably return to my business and implement what I learned with high hopes, only to experience repeated frustration and disappointment as my efforts made not the slightest difference whatsoever in my new client acquisition results.

My inability to source effective marketing methods from experts meant I had to sit down and figure it out myself, virtually from scratch.

And that's the benefit that I am passing on to you in this book: a method that is fresh, authentic, proven effective and free of all the manipulative BS that you've been told you need to engage in to generate quality new client inquiries.

By the way, the story of paying good money to marketing experts on multiple occasions, only to have nothing to show for it, is the same story I hear repeatedly from my new clients. It's very likely your experience as well.

Most of my clients experienced the same disappointment and frustration that I experienced, having paid money to people who all essentially said the same thing, "Trust me, give me your money and I'll show you how to get new clients on board."

That experience of paying for pure BS or for ineffective marketing methods is so widespread that I felt compelled to call out that out and to share what I found actually works (shock) as explicitly as I can, within the covers of a book.

How this book will help you

I believe that the following statement is a fair description of a "slice in time" that illuminates how your life will change when you implement the model I'm going to lay out in this book.

You will wake up Monday morning and, while sipping your coffee, you open your calendar for the week and you feel a warm smile spread across your face as you see bookings from prospective ideal clients who have logged appointments to meet with you so they can confirm that working with you is the right thing to do.

You are smiling because those bookings have come in; you haven't had to chase anyone or follow them up with emails or leave voice messages hoping to hear back from them.

Further, each person made their booking, aware of your fees, and they've confirmed that they have the money to work with you.

And each one has also confirmed that, provided you agree to work together; they are ready to get started.

It gets even better: there's been no significant cost in generating these inquiries and no advertising costs either online or offline, no affiliate or commission fees, and you haven't had to do any cold calling or attend any networking meetings or engage in the wishing and hoping and praying game called social media marketing.

At this point I am tempted to say, "but wait there's more," because it really does truly get even better.

You haven't had to endure headaches the result from setting up complicated online funnels and in fact you generated all those leads in literally one hour, the week before.

Also, this is not a one-off experience.

The new client inquiries are relentless: they come in week after week and month after month and year after year.

To the point where, at some stage, you may have to temporarily shut your door to new client inquiries because you've got too many new clients.

Now that's what I call a "quality problem."

This book reveals exactly how to create that scenario. It shows you step-by- step precisely how I created that reality in my own business and how I teach others through my programs to do that same thing.

I promise I won't hold anything back.

I will give you as much as I possibly can within the limited real estate of a book.

To be clear: this book is not a tease; it reveals the exact same method that, at time of writing, I've taught to hundreds of clients across 17 time zones around the world.

This brings me to another benefit of my method.

The house I live in literally rests on golden sand next to the blue ocean and white waves at little Castaways Beach in the subtropical paradise of Queensland, Australia.

And yet I generate and serve clients all around the world — without having to leave home.

I'll show you how to do that same so that, if you're an intro-vert like me, you never have to set foot outside your front door again, if that's what you want.

Equally as satisfying, I'll show you how you can generate all those new client inquiries, while still being true to your personality and your values.

And just so I'm clear, please forgive me for saying this again, because it borders on the miraculous: once you have my method set up, you'll be able to generate those new clients without significant cost or complication.

If that sounds like music to your marketing ears, then I congratulate you because investing in this book is quite likely going to be the one of the most profitable decisions that you've ever made.

Chapter One

Inbound Marketing <u>Defined</u>

The Difference Between Inbound and Outbound Marketing

In broad terms, there are two types of marketing: **inbound** and **outbound**.

However, to my great surprise when I researched for this book, I literally could not find even one effective definition that described inbound marketing as distinct from outbound.

That perhaps is an indication of how misunderstood inbound marketing is and how, for the most part, it's still an emerging science.

I'm going to define the differences between inbound and outbound marketing here but bear in mind that the context for my definitions is the marketing of professional ideas, service, and software as opposed to the marketing of physical products.

It's this context of marketing services and advice that makes my definition of inbound marketing relevant to you and that makes the actual method so effective, because it's built with that context in mind.

Engaging in inbound marketing is essential when you offer advice and services that involve the prospect entering into a relationship with you as the provider, as distinct from marketing a transaction or commodity such as a washing machine.

With a washing machine, the prospect's greatest concern is the quality of the washing machine.

With advice or services, it's the "quality" of you that they must determine.

And that distinction makes a word of difference to how you go about your marketing.

With that in mind, here are my definitions:

> **Outbound marketing** is where you invite someone to reach out and talk to you about becoming a client, or to invest in your service, *before* you know if they have an interest in working with you.

> **Inbound marketing** is where you invite someone to reach out and talk to you about becoming a client, or to invest in your service, *after* you know they have an interest in working with you.

In addition:

> **Inbound marketing** is where you offer an experience of your service before you invite a prospect to inquire or buy.

> **Outbound marketing** is where you invite prospects to inquire or buy your services without first offering them a quality experience of your brand.

<u>NOTE</u>: It's the sequence of your marketing and the timing of your offer that determines whether a marketing method is inbound or outbound. The medium through which you make your offer (online or offline, via social media or a paid advertisement) does not determine whether a method is inbound or outbound; it's the sequence that makes the difference.

If at the first point of contact, say in a direct-mail piece or at a networking meeting, you make an offer for a prospect to meet with you and talk about working together, then you're engaging in outbound marketing and you're almost certain to fail for the simple reason that you have engaged in the equivalent of proposing marriage before you've even had a first date. In fact, based on my thirty-nine years of experience, you've got a three percent chance of getting the meeting you asked for, **at best**. And that's just getting the meeting. That's not a sale.

If, however, you make that same offer *after* you have established that a prospect is interested in <u>your</u> services, and *after* they know how <u>you</u> work with your clients, and *after* they know what <u>your</u> fees are, and *after* they've confirmed that the timing would be great for them to start working with you, and *after* they understand that what you offer is unique, and *after* they believe that you are their best option, THEN and only then, have you engaged in effective inbound marketing and you have a seventy percent chance of that person becoming a client, **at worst**.

That's a helluva difference: a three percent chance of getting a meeting at best, versus a seventy percent probability of engaging a new client, at worst.

(And did you notice that engaging in outbound marketing gives you a "chance" whereas inbound give you a "probability"? I know which one I prefer.)

To be clear: whether a method is inbound or outbound has absolutely nothing to do *how* you make an offer. It has everything to do with *when* you make that offer.

Inbound marketing takes longer to get a prospect to make an inquiry, but it generates many more inquiries of high quality when it's done the way I describe in this book. Inbound marketing is worth the extra effort because it's so much more effective.

In this book, I'll give you the exact sequence and the exact right time to make your offer and I'll also show you exactly how to make that offer.

But in the meantime, I want to reinforce my point that, contrary to what many "experts" will tell you, the medium through which you make your offer does not determine whether that offer is an inbound or an outbound offer.

For example, some people will tell you that if someone clicks through to your website through a Google search or by clicking on a Google advert, then that's an example of inbound marketing.

But that's not necessarily true.

If that person, knowing nothing about you previously, clicks on the link to your website and after a little poking around they see your offer to "Book A Free Strategy Session," that isn't inbound marketing — not even close. Because you are, metaphorically speaking, proposing to meet and talk about getting married before that person has even met you. Good luck with that plan!

But let's say that same person finds your website in the same way and, once on your website, they are offered something free but something that's also very valuable in, say, the form of an e-book or a webinar.

And let's say that item proves your capability by giving them valuable and useable advice to the point where you have established rapport, respect, relatability, and reciprocity with them.

And let's say that they are *then* offered an opportunity to meet and chat about whether you can help them; *then* you've got yourself some inbound marketing.

More on how to achieve all of that shortly.

The 100 Sleeping Bears

I offered an analogy in my last book, *Marketing the Invisible*, that perfectly describes the difference between inbound and outbound marketing.

It's worth repeating here.

Imagine a forest in which there are one hundred sleeping Grizzly Bears and imagine also that you have it on good authority that exactly three of those bears have gone to sleep feeling very hungry.

And imagine that you have a pot of honey and you really want the three hungry bears to eat your honey.

If you haven't already guessed it, in this analogy the bears are a metaphor for potential ideal clients and the honey is a metaphor for your service, advice, or software. You want the bears to eat your honey; you want clients to consume your service.

You have a couple of options to achieve your objective.

The first option is to find a very large stick with a sharp point and to go running through the forest to find a sleeping bear.

Once you've found a bear, you thrust your sharp stick in the bears backside, and it wakes up snarling and swinging its big bear claws in the general direction of your head.

Having enraged the bear, you hope like crazy that it's one of the hungry ones because if it is, then the bear's hunger is likely to exceed its anger and it will eat your honey and not you.

On the other hand, if it's not one of the three hungry bears then you better be a real fast runner.

If running fast is not your thing, then I have good news: there's an alternative to rubbing 97 bears up the wrong way to find the three that are ready to eat your honey.

You simply put your honey pot outside the forest and the three hungry bears will probably start dreaming they are swimming in honey and then they'll wake up and realize they were just dreaming.

But they'll also smell your honey and they'll walk out of that forest to find your honey pot and they'll start eating your honey.

Mission accomplished.

And with much less effort, zero stress, and little risk.

The first part of my analogy is a perfect example of outbound marketing. You interrupted the bears. And 97% didn't want to be interrupted. Only 3% welcomed your offer.

And of course, the second part of the analogy perfectly illustrates what quality inbound marketing does: it allows people who have an interest in what you've got to consume a sample and thereby let you know that they have an interest in your services.

The problem with outbound marketing

The reason you need to avoid any form of outbound marketing is because it fails to acknowledge one simple truth, which is that people will want to get to know you before they'll consider reaching out and booking a time to talk with you about working together, let alone signing up with you and handing over their hard-earned money.

Except for sociopaths and narcissists, we are genetically wired to avoid feeling the stress that arises from rejection. And not only do we not like to feel rejected, we also prefer to avoid the stress that comes from rejecting others.

This means that people won't want to book a time to discuss working with you unless they are confident that they want to work with you *before* they book that call.

Unless they feel a high level of confidence in your ability, and a commensurately low level of risking of having to reject you, then their unconscious mind will move them away from booking a time to talk with you.

You and I know that that's not a particularly rational mindset; but regardless, it's the reality of how most people are unconsciously thinking.

And it's always more profitable to work with reality as it is rather than to work with it as we think it should be.

What this means is that with most of your prospects, you'll need to establish a high level of rapport and respect for your professional ability in their mind *before* you offer them the opportunity to book a time to meet with you and explore the possibility of working together.

And that's the big problem with outbound marketing: it makes the offer for the prospect to work with you prior to you having the opportunity to create those critical twin attributes of *rapport* and *respect* in their mind.

Cascading out of that deficiency are all the other reasons why you should not engage in outbound marketing. Because "premature proposition" is at the core of outbound marketing, it's inherently inefficient, expensive, and pitifully ineffective.

Can outbound marketing work?

Sure, even a blind squirrel finds an acorn in a forest occasionally.

But the infrequency and the uncertainty of finding that acorn is why you should avoid any form of outbound marketing.

There is another important reason why you should never engage in outbound marketing and that is that it saps the magnetism of your brand.

Human psychology is such that when people perceive that you need them, their reactions range from apathy to aversion. I am not a psychologist and I would not even begin to suggest *why* this is true, but after 39 years in sales and marketing, I know that it *is* true.

We can see this played out in a dating scenario where one person is very keen and exhibits symptoms of neediness and the other person stops returning calls and cuts off contact. The perception of needing new clients (as opposed to wanting new clients), is ironically enough in itself to repel inquiries from the very people you want to work with.

When you engage in outbound marketing you are signaling to the marketplace that you are in need and you should therefore not be surprised if the response is either apathy or aversion.

That in itself, apart from the fact that outbound marketing offers a very poor return for the resources consumed, should be enough to dissuade you from engaging in any form of outbound marketing.

Thirteen Benefits of My Leadsology®* Inbound Marketing Method

The unsurpassable benefits of my inbound marketing method include:

- Your brand and services generate a powerful **magnet-like appeal** to your ideal clients.

- The right prospects will rightly perceive you as **unique and indispensable.**

- New client inquiries have **pre-confirmed that they have the money** to work with you.

- Before you meet with a prospect, they will have indicated **a strong desire to work with you.**

- Every prospect will have confirmed that the **timing is good for them to start** working with you.

- Each person who makes an enquiry will be **pre-educated on how you work with your clients.**

- You will have **no need for sales techniques.**

- New clients **will pay you more** than your competitors.

- Clients will **stay longer.**

- Clients will **buy more often.**

- You can **generate high quality inquires predictably.**

- These inquiries **will flow into your business** week in and week out.

- Once set, you will generate these inquiries **without significant cost or complication**.

The problem with most inbound marketing

So having hopefully convinced you that outbound marketing is a seriously bad idea, it must also be acknowledged that inbound marketing is like any other profession or trade in the world in that it can be done exceptionally well (see above for what that looks like) and exceptionally poorly.

In the next chapter, I'll walk you through the most frequently recommended forms of marketing, most of which are inbound, and I'll identify the ones that you have probably already tried. I'll then explain why they haven't worked.

* Leadsology® is the registered trademark of my inbound marketing method.

CHAPTER TWO

Sixteen Marketing Methods You May Have Tried and Why They Haven't Worked

INTRODUCTION

I DON'T RECOMMEND MOST marketing methods, other than my form of inbound marketing, for one of four reasons.

Either:

A. They are ineffective relative to my method.

B. They are expensive relative to my method.

C. They are complicated relative to my method.

D. Refer to all three of the above i.e. they are ineffective and unnecessarily costly and complicated.

I'm painfully aware that by stating the truth this starkly I run the risk of you thinking that I am a supremely arrogant self-serving egotist, and I get that.

I'm prepared to take that risk however, because you've invested in this book and I therefore feel a responsibility to run that risk in the interests of saving you the years of wasted time, effort, and money that I endured in uncovering what didn't work and why.

Having said that, marketing is like life in that there are almost no absolutes.

For example, if I recommend that you steer clear of Facebook advertising (which I do) because it's too complicated and too expensive and it produces poor-quality leads; that's not to say that it can never work for anyone at any time or that it *always* produces leads that are expensive and of poor quality.

So, let me put it like this: as the provider of professional services or advice, relying on any of the following marketing methods is like betting your business on a pair of twos during a poker game. It's not that you can *never* win; it's just that it's *extremely unlikely* and it's *certain* that you can't repeat that win, time and again.

By contrast, the method that I recommend later in this book is like betting on a hand with four Kings. You are going to win ninety-nine times out of a hundred.

With that in mind, let's have a look at each of these most frequently recommended marketing methods and I'll share with you which of the above four reasons is why you should avoid them.

Facebook Advertising

The Holy Grail of marketing is that you do practically no work, but you have a flood of clients beating down your door wanting to pay you money.

The value proposition behind Facebook advertising is not far from that scenario.

The promise made is often that you can set up an automated, systemized advertising campaign that carefully targets only your ideal clients. A a series of landing pages, lead magnet, tripwires, segments, and auto-responders then has prospects progressing their way through a "funnel" which takes them from opting-in to your email list for something that's free, all the way through to buying a premium-priced service from you.

The promise implies that you only have to split test the steps mentioned above, figure out which side of the split test (e.g. two different advertisements, two different landing pages, two different lead magnets etc.) is the winner, kill off the loser, and replace it with a challenger to your champion.

You simply measure the number of impressions each side of the split test receives, measure pay-per-click rates, opt-in percentages, bounce rates, unique visits, duration on page and a few other metrics. Refine, tweak. and go again.

Once you get that right, you can, according to the sellers of these programs and courses, sit on a tropical beach in paradise for 30 minutes a day and let all the money wash over your beautiful body while you sip a Pina Colada and sign autographs.

Did you detect that I feel a little bit cynical about Facebook advertising and online funnels? You bet I am.

I started running Facebook advertising and developing online funnels in 2009. I ran them profitably for many years, but I stopped running them in 2016 because the quality of the leads was going down every year as the cost of acquiring those leads was going up.

For example, in 2009 I could get an email subscriber opt-in from a Facebook advertisement for a dollar each. By 2016, that was over $10 and heading north.

I still remember the day that I closed my Facebook advertising account.

I had just logged in to my online email database and I saw 869 new email subscribers who had opted in using the method I'm going to describe in this book.

I knew from experience they were of relatively high quality since they'd come from someone else's email list and had therefore opted in twice (once to the other person's email list and once to mine) registering their interest in learning more about lead generation.

I was pleased with that. Generating 869 new email subscribers is a very significant achievement.

Added to the quality and the volume of those leads was the fact that I did not pay even one cent for those new subscribers. No advertising fees, no affiliate fees, no nothing.

After seeing that result, I can recall then opening my Facebook advertising account and seeing that I owed over $3,000 to Mark Zuckerberg (the founder of Facebook) for one month of advertising.

That one month had generated a little under 300 new email subscribers and I knew from decades of experience that the likelihood of one of those subscribers buying from me was a quarter of one percent compared to three percent from the 869 new email subscribers that I had generated for free.

Face with the same facts, what would you have done?

On the one hand I was paying thousands of dollars every month for a marketing method that was very complicated to set up and that delivered relatively poor-quality subscribers.

On the other hand, I could generate almost three times the volume of email subscribers who were approximately 12 times more likely to buy from me and I was doing that for completely zero cost.

It's a bit of a no-brainer, right?

Almost everyone who I have spoken to who has tried Facebook advertising and setting up online funnels has come to exactly the same conclusion: it's a very expensive, very complicated method for generating very poor-quality leads.

So if you bought some fancy-pants software or signed up to some "you-beaut" platform that promises that it is all going to be easy and simple and highly profitable, then I'm telling you from experience (mine and many others) to cut your losses, get whatever money you can back again, and walk away.

That might seem tough but it's advice that will potentially save you thousands upon thousands of dollars and hundreds of wasted hours together with incalculable levels of frustration and disappointment.

Other than that, Facebook advertising online funnels are great. (Yes, that's a cynical sign off).

MAINSTREAM MEDIA ADVERTISING

Mainstream media advertising is a complete waste of money when you're marketing professional services or advice, and it's largely (although not completely) a waste of money if you're marketing software.

(A note on marketing software: At some point or another over the last four decades I've successfully marketed pretty much everything. In the first 20 years or so of my career, I was selling or marketing either physical products or services. Then along came software. The way I see it, software is not really a physical thing, but neither is it completely invisible. So it sits in between the physical and the service-type products. But software mostly needs to be marketed in a manner which is more similar to the marketing of services and advice, than the marketing of physical products.)

On the subject of using radio, television, newspapers and magazines (be they online or off-line), I've tried them all.

I often say to my clients that my job is to waste tens of thousands of dollars and hundreds of hours on attempting marketing that fails, so that they don't have to.

So yes, I burned a lot of money trying to get advertising in mainstream media working, but I would have been better off if I'd taken half of the advertising budget in cash and flushed it down the toilet and kept the other half. It would have saved me a lot of time and I would have had more money left in my bank account too.

When it comes to generating new client inquiries, as opposed to brand building (which for small businesses I am vehemently opposed to), advertising doesn't work for the simple reason that you are not selling a washing machine or a set of golf clubs, but rather a relationship.

Other than mail order brides, no one got married on the basis of a fancy-pants billboard or radio advertisement. And it's the same deal if you're offering services that require your prospect to enter into a longer-term relationship with you.

The three-step marketing method that I will reveal later in this book is infinitely more effective than any form of advertising and it will cost you precisely nothing in advertising costs or affiliate fees or commissions.

So again, like the Facebook advertising, why would anyone in their right mind want to waste money trying to get mainstream media advertising working, when there is a fee-free alternative that produces a much higher volume and much higher quality of leads?

The answer is that they wouldn't, other than they don't know about the inbound alternative in this book.

Also, there is no shortage of advertising agencies or media representatives who will tell you that advertising is the answer to your marketing prayers.

And it's true that mainstream media advertising can be very effective if you're marketing physical products such as property or vehicles or sporting equipment. In fact, I'd go so far as to say that if you're marketing physical products, it would be a smart move to find an advertising medium and format that's effective.

Finally, the reason that people waste money on advertising is that it represents a potential shortcut to fixing their marketing challenges.

Some people prefer to throw money at a marketing method because it saves them the time and trouble of trying to figure it all out. And in the absence of a method that they know does actually work, I can't really blame them.

BUSINESS NETWORKING MEETINGS

I have a pathological hatred of going to business networking meetings. Some people love them and if that's you, then I encourage you to keep going.

But I'm an introvert and I find a lot of my clients prefer a computer screen to shaking hands and smiling at people they have never met before.

My wife is the opposite. At our wedding, I had one friend attend and she had around 50.

Recently, when a wildfire was threatening our home and we were told to prepare to evacuate, she received some 23 offers of accommodation via SMS or social media.

I received precisely none. (Perversely enough, I'm quite proud of that.)

The reason for sharing that with you is to acknowledge my social deficiencies which only served to underline my resistance to going to business networking meetings.

Having provided you with that disclosure, and now putting it aside, let's look at the idea of going to business networking meetings with the objective of generating new client inquiries.

If you have a local business such as a local accountancy firm, a plumbing or electrical firm, and you are restricted in the provision of services to clients to your local geographical area, then by all means attend the business networking meetings because they can indeed be highly profitable.

If, however, you wish to position yourself as an expert who is in demand then you will do yourself a great disservice by trotting along to your local business networking meeting and handing out your business cards in the hope that people might want to do business with you.

The funny thing about us humans is that we prefer to get our advice from people who are in demand.

In fact, there is no reason why someone who is not in demand is necessarily a worse option, but we unconsciously equate demand with quality.

Therefore, if you go to business networking meetings or you set up a stand at a trade show, you are inviting your target market to respond on a spectrum that ranges from apathy or aversion because you're signaling that, rather than being in a state of demand, you are in a state of need.

But let's assume that, unlike me, you enjoy going to business networking meetings and let's assume also that you offer a professional service or advice and you understand the risks of de-powering the attractiveness and appeal of your services by flagging to everyone present that you're on the lookout for more business.

And let's be even more generous and assume that the first couple of meetings that you attend, you are given some referrals which you follow-up and, by some miracle (refer to the "blind squirrel in a forest finding an acorn once in a while"), one of those leads becomes a client.

That can happen.

But will that happen week in and week out for years to come?

Definitely not.

That's because you're going back to a group that consists of 80% of the same people week in, week out. They are going to run out of referrals for you fast. It's like fishing in a small pond; it's not going to take long before you've over-fished the resource.

Then you have not only de-powered your brand, but you are also not getting any leads and you're pretty much just wasting your time.

If, however, you treat the business networking meetings as a socially enjoyable outing, and you're okay with the impact it has on your brand, then you should keep doing it.

And I *am* serious about that: if you enjoy business networking and tradeshows, keep doing them.

There's not an *enormous* amount of downside and I'm a big fan of doing stuff that's enjoyable.

A Marketing Program or Course

I like programs and courses. Workshops and seminars too. They can be interesting, and I always learn something.

Unfortunately, from a pure commercial profit point of view, the programs and courses and workshops and seminars that I've invested in have mostly failed to deliver tangible, measurable, and significant improvement in my results.

I'm not saying they are a waste of time. I still invest in them when I can find one that looks interesting or promises a modicum of profit.

What I am saying, however, is they rarely generate a measurable financial return on investment.

The exceptions tend to be those programs and courses that either offer an unconditional money-back guarantee of satisfaction, or better still, the ones that ask you to pay after you've experienced them.

I appreciate that the latter category in particular are very rare, but if you follow the method that I outline later in this book you will see why it's profitable to offer your prospects to work with you before they pay you any money. But more on that later.

In the meantime, I'd encourage you to keep doing the programs and courses but to understand that, in the majority of cases, it'll be an educational experience which, while beneficial in the long term, may not be particularly profitable in the short term. That's the way I approach them.

BUSINESS COACHES

One out of ten business coaches is fantastic.

What happens when you get one of the others is that you work with them and pay them each month and at some point between the third and sixth month, you send them the "Dear John" email.

In the email, you explain to your coach that "it's not you, it's me," and you tell them that they've been wonderful but that you "just need to put things on hold for a while," which is code language for "you ain't never seeing me again."

In other words, you pay month after month, but some point between the third and sixth payment, you decide that you need to politely part company because you are not seeing any results.

If only the one out of ten business coaches that is effective would walk around with a sign on their head. But alas they don't.

If you get a great business coach, then stick with him or her.

Frankly, regardless of whether or not they can help you specifically with your marketing (which they rarely can), they can be worth every cent because they will put processes, platforms, and people in place and that alone will support the development of your business.

MASTERMIND GROUPS

These are similar to business coaches.

A small percentage of Mastermind Groups will provide you with a very significant return on the exorbitant fees that they mostly charge, but most of them won't.

Here's how the mastermind group experience plays out.

You sign up for a year and you attend the meetings and the guy or gal running the meeting is really swell and other members seem to be getting value, but not you.

So you don't renew.

You put it down to experience and you think "maybe it was just me."

But it's not.

The big problem for mastermind groups is turnover.

Churn.

Normally, it's because the leader of the group gets lazy and expects the mastermind members to add value to each other instead of stepping up to the plate and providing fresh and effective content throughout the year.

I'm not against mastermind groups. When I was last running them, I had four separate groups running simultaneously and the numbers in those groups ranged from 25 to 140 each.

And my renewal rate of members from year one to year two was 75% and the renewal rate from year two to year three was 90% and many stayed for between five and seven years.

One of the reasons for my success with running mastermind groups was that I delivered fresh and valuable content at every single meeting, without any exception.

From my point of view, running masterminds was a highly profitable exercise. But I stopped doing them for a bunch of reasons, but partly because I just got tired of running them.

If you find a great mastermind group that is being led by a leader who steps up to the plate and delivers fresh and effective content to you on a regular basis, then stick with it.

And there are a few of them around. It's just that I haven't personally found one yet despite continuing to try.

The bottom line with mastermind groups is that most people find that they are not receiving enough value to justify the investment from one year to the next, or to sustain the time and effort involved in travel and attendance.

TRADESHOWS

You'll most likely have read above my comments about attending business networking meetings and why I don't attend them, which is because I'm an antisocial, introverted hermit and going to such meetings is, in my mind at least, akin to running up the white flag of surrender in regard to positioning my brand as one that is in demand.

I recently accidentally won a prize to speak at a large conference and a part of the prize was the offer of setting up a booth at the conference's ancillary tradeshow. I say "accidentally" because I had no idea I had even entered a competition. I was simply supporting a colleague's promotion because it looked like a worthwhile offer for my subscribers.

Having won the opportunity to set up a stall at the trade show, I told the organizer that I'd prefer to dangle my testicles on the electric fence at the back of our property for an hour rather than attend a booth in a trade show for five minutes.

You might be able to pick up from that that I'm not a big fan of standing in a booth handing out brochures or asking people to put their business cards into a big glass bowl for a prize draw.

Once again, the reasons are similar to why I don't attend business networking meetings. It de-powers my brand because I'm asking my market to "pick me." The psychology of attraction does not work like that.

Note that the exception to my position on trade shows would be for those of my clients who are software developers. That's because software is the most scalable product on the planet. You can make it once and have 1 million people using it simultaneously (in most cases), so the concept of running out of supply because there was so much demand doesn't work the same as it does with services or advice.

REFERRALS

I love referrals. Someone emails me and says they were referred by a client and that they want to talk about working with me.

Mostly they are pre-educated about how I work with my clients and they are pre-motivated because my client said some kind words to them about the effectiveness of my program.

So it's an easy conversation to have and the inquiry has been generated with literally zero effort and at no cost.

What's not to like about referrals?

In order to answer that question, let me just point out that there are two types of referrals. Solicited an unsolicited.

If you have a referral *system* in place, and I recommend that you do, then you'll generate more referrals than if you don't have a referral system in place.

I guess that's pretty obvious.

The downside of having a referral system in place where your clients are regularly asked for referrals is that, while you'll generate more referrals than if you don't have a system in place, those referrals are going to be of lower quality than the second type of referral, which is the unsolicited one.

The unsolicited referrals are commonly known as "word-of-mouth" referrals.

The problem with word-of-mouth referrals is that you can't push a button or pull a lever and have them flow in.

You have to sit and wait and pray and hope.

Will they come in?

Absolutely.

But you don't know when so you can't budget for them coming in.

If you own your own business, then your future financial security and prosperity is dependent on clients paying you money. The idea of course is that you take some of that money out of your business and create personal wealth and financial independence.

But if you can't control the flow of new client inquiries, then you can't control the flow of new client payments and you therefore have no control over your financial future. That's scary.

The bottom line here is twofold.

Firstly, by all means have a referral system in place but understand that the quality of those referrals will not be as high as word-of-mouth referrals. The more you ask for referrals, the greater the volume that will flow, but the poorer the quality.

Secondly, whilst word-of-mouth referral is fabulous when it happens, you can't depend on it and so you need an inbound marketing method that will generate high-quality, inbound new client inquiries whenever you need them, regardless of whatever referrals come your way.

In my marketing world, referrals are simply the cream on my proverbial new client cake. Nice to have but not essential.

LinkedIn

I make a lot of money out of LinkedIn and I show selected clients how to do the same.

LinkedIn is a gold mine. There's no doubt about that.

However, LinkedIn does not work the way that almost all of the sales trainers tell you that it works.

Most LinkedIn experts will tell you that the first thing you need to do is figure out your ideal client profile and start getting first level connections with those people. That part the experts have right.

It's what they recommend next which doesn't work.

Which is that they recommend that you post regular content that's going to be perceived as valuable by your LinkedIn connections or the LinkedIn Group you started up or are a member of.

Recommendations vary, but most will advise that you post an article or a video each week over a 90-day period and that will build your brand in the recipient's brain. After the 90-day period, you should point out that you're available to talk about their needs, relative to the services or advice that you're offering.

The reason I know that this doesn't work is that I've tried it and spent many thousands of dollars and hundreds of hours trying to make it work. And I am a professional marketer.

To be fair to all the LinkedIn trainers out there who are recommending the above method, I thought it would work as well.

After all, it works when people subscribe to my email list. They receive regular and valuable content and I thereby keep my brand in their brain until they are ready to buy.

So when the same method of nurturing a contact that worked so well with my email list didn't work with LinkedIn connections, I set out to find why email subscribers responded completely differently than LinkedIn connections.

Here is my conclusion: LinkedIn connections have the complete reverse order of priority than email subscribers.

Email subscribers opt in to my email list because they are first and foremost interested in the benefit of my services. Once they've established that there may be benefit in engaging with my services, they then seek to validate my integrity in regard to how well I can deliver on my promises. Therefore, email subscribers have as their first priority the benefit of my services. Their second priority is me.

As mentioned, LinkedIn connections order of priority is completely in reverse.

Think about it. In broad terms, there are three categories of people who are on LinkedIn and there is no fourth category.

The first category of LinkedIn members is the Head Hunters or recruitment agents.

They are looking for talent they can place with the client's organization.

The second category of the Head Huntees keep their LinkedIn profile up-to-date and nice and shiny just in case the Head Hunters contact them with a better job offer.

The third category of LinkedIn members is those people who want to sell you something or want to use your network to sell them something.

The fourth category that consists of precisely nobody are the people who wake up in the morning and think "oh goody, I'll log into my LinkedIn account and maybe someone will sell me something."

And when I say "nobody" I'm pretty sure that's about right.

So assuming that you're not in the Head Hunter or Head Huntee categories, so I'll conclude that you've joined LinkedIn in the hope of selling someone something.

The problem is that almost all your connections have joined for exactly the same reason.

Everyone is running abound LinkedIn trying to avoid being seen to be "selling" something while at the same time trying to sell something.

To each other!

It's really quite comical.

That little circus aside, what this means is that, first and foremost, your LinkedIn connections are interested first and foremost in you and not your services.

As noted above, this order of interest is the complete reverse of the order of interest of your email subscribers.

Nurturing email subscribers with high-quality content on a regular basis works well because the content you're publishing fulfils their priority need, which is for valuable information related to your service.

But with LinkedIn, people are not primarily connected with you for the purpose of finding out more about your services, but rather they are connected with you in the hope that they can sell you something or that you can introduce them to people who they can sell to.

So, if you're posting regular content to LinkedIn with the hope of generating new client inquiries, I can save you a lot of time and effort and frustration and disappointment by telling you not to.

Again, refer to my comments about blind squirrels in forests finding an acorn once in a while.

But even if you do generate a new client by posting content to LinkedIn, it's not a dependable, systematic, predictable, relentless system for generating high-quality, inbound new client inquiries.

So, don't do it. At least not the way most people tell you to do it. I'll show you later how to mine the gold in LinkedIn without posting a single added-value post.

Just to drive home the random and futile nature of posting content to LinkedIn, the last time I checked with LinkedIn, 7,222 articles were being posted to that platform every hour.

Of every day.

Of every week.

Of ever year.

That's over 100 new articles every minute.

Your article, should you choose to post one, is literally "gone in 60 seconds" and is buried under an avalanche of other articles within a fraction of even that short period of time.

Finally, I'm not saying that you should never post content to LinkedIn.

My Social Media Manager posts content there pretty much every week of the year.

But we don't do that with the intention of generating new clients.

We do it simply because it takes only one click of a mouse button to post links to content that has been created for other purposes. I'm happy to be that blind squirrel but I sure as heck am not going to rely on posting content to LinkedIn to generate a *predictable flow* of new client inquiries.

Blogging or Podcasting

This one's easy.

It's certainly possible to generate new client inquiries through blogging and podcasting.

All you need to do is publish high-quality, valuable content, two to three times a week over five years and you'll get a pretty reliable flow of new client inquiries.

Yep: about five years.

I'm not saying don't do it. I have a blog and a podcast.

But like posting to LinkedIn, I don't do it with any expectation of generating new client inquiries. I do it for the purposes of nurturing our email list with good quality content and for SEO (search engine optimization) purposes.

NEW WEBSITE

I don't know why but there are a lot of people out there who think a new website is going to be the solution to their marketing problems, or at least a significant part of the solution.

There's a whole new science around the subject of website visitors' behavior or UX (user experience).

It's fascinating. I don't pretend to understand it to the extent that I could offer sage or effective advice on the subject, but I am a keen student.

In fact, I've just hired not one, but two UX consultants to review our website and come up with a better way of capturing the contact details of visitors, in exchange for offering them valuable content.

I currently achieve that objective to a satisfactory degree, but I'm quite sure we can do a whole lot better.

That said, I get thousands of unique visitors to my website every month (www.leadsology.guru). So I have something to convert.

And that's the problem for most people who think that a new website is the answer.

They simply don't have enough traffic yet to warrant the investment in developing a new website.

If you have a few dozen unique visitors to your website every month then you don't need to invest in a new website. You need to invest in building an email list and generating clients from that email list.

This book will show you how to do that.

The vast majority of people who spend thousands of dollars on a new website are the personification of the metaphorical equivalent of erecting a billboard with neon lights in the middle of the Sahara Desert.

It doesn't matter how great it looks if no one sees it, in which case it's simply a big fat waste of money.

And web-presence is far more important than web-site.

Social Media Marketing

The term "social media marketing" is an oxymoron. It's a contradiction in terms.

I'll keep this brief in order to save you time and in the hope that you'll believe me.

Social Media is fabulous for keeping your Brand in people's Brains until they're ready to Buy. I call that BBB.

But they won't buy professional services simply because you posted a pic or video on Instagram.

You will need some form of Call To Action (more on that later) so that, when they are ready to buy, they will know how to do that.

We post to all major social media platforms more than once a week. But just like blogging or podcasting, I'm not expecting new client inquiries to flow as a result of those posts.

Once again, by all means post to Social Media, but please understand that while it does a terrific job of BBB, it does an absolutely lousy job of getting people to buy.

Social Media is simply not designed to make sales.

PR

PR can stand for press release or public relations. There is some crossover between the two, but they generally result in the same thing, which is a big fat nothing.

I've appeared on radio talkback shows, on breakfast television, and I've been featured in magazines and newspapers but not so much in recent years for the simple reason that the dollars and hours invested bring me a better result elsewhere.

Generating inbound leads is not simply about visibility.

Yes, it's true that unless you get noticed nobody's going buy anything.

But it is the *way* that you get noticed *and* the opportunity to make an offer that makes the difference.

PR is a bit like social media. It's not a medium which is explicitly designed for you to make a Call To Action.

Without exception, every person who has told me they have engaged a public relations consultant to get them exposure had a remarkably similar experience to my own, which was that it was all a lot of fun and very exciting, but spectacularly unproductive.

AGENCIES

There are two reasons why, when it comes to your marketing, you should not put all your eggs in the agency basket.

The first one is that in excess of 95% of the time they'll simply take your money, say things that make sense and soothe your concerns, but that after three months of handing over your hard-earned cash, you'll conclude that it is simply not generating even a breakeven result for you. It's the same experience that most people have with most business coaches (refer #5 above).

If you're a very patient person, you might even stretch that to six months before you politely fire the agency.

And then the agency goes and finds someone else who has the same hopes and dreams and aspirations that you had when you hired them.

Agencies operate like the revolving doors at a big department store. New clients are flowing on in while the old ones are flowing on out. The only difference is that, with most Agencies, the old clients are walking out empty-handed. At least with department stores they walk out with bags or shiny things.

Of course, just like business coaches and mastermind groups, there are rare exceptions.

The common denominator with agencies that take your money and deliver zero return on investment is that they want money up front.

If you suggest that you pay them out of results, they will quickly walk away because they have zero confidence in their ability to get you results.

The second reason why you should not put all your eggs in the agency basket applies only if you manage to find an agency that actually delivers a significant and measurable return on your investment.

By the way, if that happens, then please let me know; I'll hire them tomorrow.

But even if I found an effective agency that gave me a significant return on investment, I would never allow myself to become dependent on them to generate any more than one third of my new business flows.

That's because, if I were to do that, I would be creating a dependency that would make the success of my business vulnerable to their failure.

That's just not smart.

We all know that when it comes to financial investments, diversity increases security.

It's exactly the same with your marketing. Don't put all your eggs in one agency basket —even if it is delivering great results (unlikely, but I'll keep looking).

The way you can tell if you've found an effective agency is if they are prepared for you to pay *after* they have generated revenue for you.

If they are not prepared to make that offer, then don't pay them a brass cent.

APPOINTMENT-SETTERS

Appointment-setters make appointments for you with people who are allegedly interested in buying your services. To get those appointments booked for you, they will often message LinkedIn contacts or send out thousands of emails, spam or otherwise.

One of their redeeming features is that they only charge you for appointments that they set up. Hence "appointment setters."

Sounds good, right?

They set you up with say ten appointments every week for people to meet with you and talk about your services.

And you only pay them when they set those appointments up.

How can you lose on a deal like that?

Actually, you lose quite easily.

Firstly, out of every ten appointments set, only five show up.

Of those five, four are broke and the fifth one wants to "think about it" which is code language for one of two things.

Either "I'm going to shop around" or "no."

Either way, they never get back to you. And when I say "never" I actually mean "never, ever, ever."

Meantime, you are out of pocket for $500 ($50 for every appointment that was set) and you've wasted five hours, plus the down time for the no-shows and you're now feeling frustrated and disappointed.

Other than that, appointment-setters are great!

Unfortunately, that's how pretty much all marketing efforts end when we try to generate prospects from a poor-quality source.

List Buying

Many people make the mistake of thinking that marketing is mostly about finding the contact details of people who fit their ideal client's demographic.

For example, a financial planner targeting pre-retirees might buy a list of 10,000 names and addresses of career professionals between 55 – 65 years of age and think they now have 10,000 leads.

They don't.

What they have is 10,000 names and addresses. They still must convert that list into clients and in ignorance of Principle #1 above (Avoiding Hugh Jackman Marketing) they are doomed to fail.

The reason I mention that example is that it's representative of what many people believe, which is that finding an Audience is the answer to solving the problem of lead generation. It's a solid start but there is a critical point that would be profitable for you to note which is that…

The source of your Audience determines their likelihood of buying from you.

Buying a list of contact details is a poor-quality source because they represent the 100 Sleeping Bears I wrote about in

Chapter One, except with list-buying, the number of likely hungry bears shrinks from 3% to 0.1%.

That's not much.

And it's expensive.

CONCLUSION

I'm hopeful that you will recognize the value in what I just shared with you.

It took me eleven years and I wasted tens of thousands of dollars in figuring this stuff out.

If you do nothing else but follow my advice in respect of the above you will have received value in return for your investment in this book, in the order of tens of thousands of percentage points.

And if you feel a little depressed about all the marketing methods that are commonly taught and yet are either ineffective or too complicated or too expensive, then please don't give up hope because I am about to reveal a method that does work and that works incredibly well and without significant cost or complication.

CHAPTER THREE

The Five Principles of Effective Inbound Marketing

INTRODUCTION

A PRINCIPLE IS DEFINED as a fundamental truth or proposition.

A prescription is a recommended solution.

Principles are timeless. Prescriptions change.

In principle it's advantageous to be able to move from one place to another.

The original prescription for that was called walking or running. That prescription was added to with bicycles, trains, automobiles, planes and rocket ships.

But the principle never changed. Only the variety of prescriptions.

The principle of eating nutritious food in order to enjoy high energy and good health, hasn't changed.

The prescription of what nutritious food consists of, has changed.

We've gone from what was very likely a diet of mostly meat and a handful of nuts and berries to a prescription that adds fruit, vegetables and grains to that mix.

Principles never change, prescriptions do.

The principle of developing skills to enhance prosperity has also been consistent from time immemorial.

But the prescription, or specific skills required, have constantly changed from being able to hunt sabre tooth tigers and woolly mammoths to becoming an I.T. expert and everything in between.

This chapter is all about the four principles of effective inbound marketing and these four principles are timeless.

The following chapters are about prescriptions.

More specifically, the chapters that follow are a three-part prescription that incorporates and honors all five principles that I'll outline in this chapter.

And while I would love to think that I will never have to change the prescription, history would suggest very strongly that I'd be a fool to believe that.

Having said that, I can tell you that the prescription or method that I offer is unlikely to change in the next 20 – 30 years and so it should survive well beyond my lifetime. That's all

I'll need it for, and it will probably send most of my clients off into happy and prosperous retirement lifestyles too.

But should you outlive my prescription, I can assure you that by understanding the five principles, you'll be able to adapt or change my prescription and still enjoy success in your inbound lead generation efforts.

PRINCIPLE #1: YOU ARE NOT HUGH JACKMAN

Readers of my previous book *Marketing the Invisible* will need to forgive me for repeating this principle. There is however a pretty good chance that even if you have read that book you may have forgotten this invaluable lesson.

In that book I tell the story of having coffee with my wife at our home when I asked her who she thought was world's most irresistible man.

"Why of course, you are sweetie" she said, with a grin and a wink.

"Yes, I know I am; I mean who could resist my bald head, pot belly and wrinkled skin? But apart from me?" I asked.

After a few half-hearted nominations and a fair bit of pressure from me she finally came up with a convincing answer.

"Ah!" she said, "I've got it! Hugh Jackman!"

"Of course!" I agreed.

"He can sing, he can dance, he can act, he's a devoted husband and family man, apparently deeply caring about all sorts of social and environmental issues. He's incredibly good looking and he's got a body that would make Adonis jealous. Plus, he's got enough money for the next 100 lifetimes."

"OK" I said. "I've got another question for you.

Imagine that there's a knock at the front door right now. You put down your coffee, you go to the door and you open it. And it's Hugh Jackman. He sees you, drops to one knee and holds up a small red velvet box and he opens it to reveal a million dollar diamond ring that sparkles in the sunlight and the first words out of his mouth are *'Hi there, you don't know me but my name is Hugh Jackman. Would you make me the happiest man on earth and marry me, and run away with me and live with me for the rest of your life?'*

What would you say to him?" I asked.

Beloved paused for a moment then this...

"Well firstly, Tom" she said, "you know that I love you, right?"

"Sure" I said, "And I think I know what you're going to say next."

"Well I'm sorry" she blurted out "but I'd run away with him!"

I thought for a moment then said "Petal, there is absolutely no need to apologize. Frankly, if *I'd* answered the door, and

Hugh was on bended knee proposing to *me,* I'd have probably run away with him too and I'm not even gay. I mean, it's Hugh freakin' Jackman!" I said.

So what's Hugh Jackman proposing to my beautiful wife got to do with you and your marketing?

Plenty.

Most people practice what I call Hugh Jackman Marketing.

They conduct their marketing as if what they have is so irresistible, so incredible, so genius-filled, that everyone they meet should instantly want to do business with them.

For example: they go to a business networking meeting with the intent of "picking up" a new client. They thrust their business cards into the hands of people they've never met before, hoping that one of them will want to work with them.

For example: they put an advertisement in a paper or magazine or online, promoting their services and hoping someone will read it and immediately make contact and inquire about becoming a client.

For example: they hope that they sit next to a high-quality prospect at their next dinner party so they'll be able to woo that person into becoming a client.

I call this Hugh Jackman Marketing because they think that they can get to an "engagement" on their first meeting. Or second or third.

Either way it comes down to the same approach: a failure to allow a prospect to get to know your work and to progressively discover how awesome you are "on the inside" because, let's face it, most of us do not possess the business equivalent of Hugh Jackman's irresistibility and our potential Ideal Clients may just need a few "dates" first and see that true beauty is more than just skin deep.

Only 20% of my bookings from people who want to talk with me about become a client come from people who had one "date" with me. They read one of my books, they attended one of my talks or webinar. Then they booked a time to talk with me.

Eighty percent have five "dates" with me prior to booking that call. Five! What a contrast to those who are practicing Hugh Jackman marketing by advertising their services and hoping people will buy like they were the commercial equivalent of the irresistible Hugh Jackman.

PRINCIPLE #2: DOGS SHOULD STICK TO BARKING

Cats wake up in the morning and are inclined to meow.

Dogs wake up in the morning and are inclined to bark.

Metaphorically speaking, you're either a cat or a dog.

In this metaphor, entrepreneurs are represented by dogs and technicians are represented by cats.

Dogs are big-picture thinkers, they enjoy strategy and they love starting things.

They have a waterfall of ideas cascading through the mind every single day. But they don't thrive on detail such as five-year cash flow spreadsheets, and as much as they love starting new things, they quickly get bored and lose interest in finishing them.

Dogs love developing products and services and they love working with clients and seeing results.

By contrast, cats love detail and they feel secure with routine and they can't sleep until the thing is finished and sorted and tidied. Whereas dogs were born to disrupt and create, cats were born to tidy up and implement.

Essentially what I'm saying is that we need to stick to our inclinations.

That's a keyword.

You will feel naturally inclined to engage in certain activities when you're at work and you'll avoid other activities.

Dogs will avoid financial meetings and cats will avoid sales calls.

You're either wired one way or another.

After 39 years in sales and marketing, I estimate that 97% of all marketing methods fail because a dog is trying to meow.

In other words, someone is trying a marketing method that they don't want to do. And so they either don't do it or they do it infrequently or they do it badly, just like a dog try to meow.

Think about it.

If you don't want to do a thing, whether it's a restrictive diet or an overly strenuous exercise regime, do you stick to it?

The answer is invariably, for the <u>vast</u> majority of us, no.

Case in point: I don't like going to the gym and working out on the treadmill, but for some 37 years I was happy to run in parks and forests and mountains and along beaches.

Personal trainers told me I should be pumping weights but instead I just ran and, while in nature at the end of my run, I'd do some push-ups and sit-ups and other strength/conditioning exercises.

I tried the gym. But I could never make it stick. I felt like a dog trying to meow.

What stuck was doing the sort of exercise I *wanted* to do which was running out in nature.

Here's the reality of marketing: you will do the sort of marketing that you *want* to do. And if you want to do it, then you'll do it a lot and you'll get better at doing it.

Let's say that you go to some seminar or attend a webinar and the presenter is telling you all about the merits of Facebook advertising and setting up online funnels (refer to item #1 in the previous chapter) and you wake up the next morning and say to yourself: "I *should* really start a Facebook advertising account and set up some funnels."

The moment you hear yourself using that word *"should,"* you're doomed.

Every day you wake up and you do things that you *want* to do.

Every day.

Only on some days do you wake up and do the things that you feel you *should* do.

Therefore, in order for a marketing method to be effective you have to *want* to do it.

Otherwise you're going to be like a dog that's been told it should meow. If you do it, then it's going to be ugly and you won't keep doing it, so it won't work.

In the prescription that I outline in the following chapters, see if you find yourself feeling that you *want* to follow my recommended method.

If you genuinely want to conduct your marketing in the manner that I recommend, then you will succeed.

Once you want to do a thing, it's simply a matter of practice until you master it.

No want, no mastery.

The cornerstone of all effective inbound marketing is that you *want* to engage in it.

Principle #3: Water Filters Work for Two Reasons

Imagine that you have some dirty stormwater and that you're thirsty and that you therefore need to figure out a way to purify the water so that you can drink it.

The solution of course is to put the water through a filtering system.

An effective water filtering system relies on two things.

First of all, it has to have enough filters of the right type for the water to pass through, capturing any toxic material and sediment and impurities, so that only pure water comes out the bottom of the filter that is safe for you to drink.

Secondly, you need a large enough volume of water, otherwise all you'll get through the filters are a couple of drips which will not be enough to satisfy your thirst and sustain your body.

Prospects are like the stormwater: they need to be filtered so that what you get is pure enough to satisfy and sustain your business needs.

If you don't have enough filters between you and the marketplace then you end up talking to people who either can't afford to work with you or who need a different service provider or solution.

And if you have the filters in place but you don't have volume then you simply don't get enough inquiries, like drips of water. Not enough to satisfy or sustain.

The principle I'm illustrating here is that every effective inbound marketing system must provide you with both the volume of leads you need, as well as the right number and type of filters, so that what you end up with is a high-quality flow of inbound, new client inquiries.

My method will show you exactly which filters you need to put in place and how to get sufficient volume passing through them. That's my promise and I'll begin revealing that in the following chapters.

PRINCIPLE #4: YOUR BOOK NEEDS A 'DIFFERENT BETTER' COVER

Imagine you've written the world's very best book on the subject matter of your specialty.

It wins all sorts of awards and is showered with praise from every expert in your industry. It's literally the very best book ever written on the subject and you're rightly gosh-darned proud of it.

Now imagine that you visit the biggest bookstore in your area in order to stand back from the shelves and see your book proudly on display.

You look at a massive wall to ceiling set of bookshelves and spot your book well-positioned, right in the middle amongst other, less superior books on the same subject.

As you stand back, you notice a shopper scanning all the books in the section where your book is on display.

He or she picks five books out of that section and carries that stack of books toward the checkout, but you're disappointed to see that your book is not one of them.

You can't help yourself: you intercept them, offer an apology for interrupting them, and ask them "do you mind if I ask you a quick question about the books you selected?"

They agree to your request and you explain that you are the author of one of the books that they overlooked and that it has been rated by every major expert as the best book in the history of mankind on the subject of their obvious interest, and you ask them why they selected the other books and not yours.

After glancing over to the bookshelves, they turn back to you and say, "I'm sorry I didn't pick your book but frankly, the covers all looked kind of the same, so I just chose some at random."

You thank them and wander back to the bookshelves and sure enough, every single book has the same cover and the same title and the same colors.

Can you blame them for not picking your book?

Absolutely not!

The genius of your book was inside the book and was not articulated on the cover, which to the uneducated observer, looked the same as all the others.

How do we judge a book?

By its cover.

Should we judge a book by its cover?

Nope.

But do we?

Absolutely!

Of course, this little story is another metaphor which in this case referred to the critical and fatal mistake of looking and sounding the same as your competitors.

If you don't stand out, then you don't get noticed.

If you don't get noticed, you don't get considered.

If you don't get considered, you don't get chosen.

For you to get noticed, you must be different.

Ideally, different as in "better different."

Even "wacky different" is better than "same."

Just look at the success of the book *The Subtle Art of Not Giving A Fxxk*. That was always going to get noticed.

But frankly, even "worse different" is better than "same." At least you get noticed.

The worst sin in marketing is being the same.

The brain of your ideal client is bombarded with marketing messages dozens of times if not hundreds of times every day and sometimes every hour.

And there is a part of every brain that is called the "Reticular Activating System," or RAS for short.

The job of your RAS is to filter the vast quantity of information fed into the unconscious mind from each of the five senses and to evaluate it in a nanosecond and decide whether or not each input should be ignored or given your attention.

You don't want your marketing message to be stored in the "same as what we already know" part of your ideal clients' brains.

Same gets ignored.

Different gets noticed.

Therefore, you must incorporate the principle of being different in order for your inbound marketing efforts to be effective.

PRINCIPLE #5: NEVER OUTSOURCE YOUR OXYGEN SUPPLY

High-quality leads flowing into your business is similar to the oxygen flowing into your body. If the flow of oxygen to your body were to be cut off, your body would die. Likewise, if the flow of leads coming into your business stops, then just like your body, your business will die. It just takes a bit longer, that's all.

There's an old saying that "nothing happens in a business until something is sold." And it is true: you can't pay your suppliers, you can't take money out of your business to pay your mortgage or rent, you can't hire people, you can't put money into research and development and so on.

However, while it's true that nothing happens in a business until something is sold, it is equally true that nothing is sold until an inquiry is generated. That's why lead generation is critical.

Given that the generation of high-quality, new client inquiries is essential not just to the survival of your business but its health and prosperity, only a fool would abdicate responsibility for the generation of those inquiries.

Here is what happens, 19 times out of 20, when you outsource your lead generation to say a Facebook agency or an advertising agency or an appointment-setting agency or any other organization that says to you: "trust me, give me your money and we'll go and generate leads for you."

You pay them some money and they get to work.

You see zero results or poor-quality leads flowing in.

But you're a patient person and they seem like nice people, so you keep paying the money month after month.

But nothing changes and because you're a nice person you send a nice email saying that you have to put things on hold for a while.

All that's changed in your business is that you transferred money from your bank account to their bank account. Other than that hole in your bank account, you have nothing to show for the trust that you placed in that third-party agency.

How do I know this to be true? Because I am one of the schmucks that handed over the money. On numerous occasions. And around 70% of my clients have the same tale of woe and waste to tell.

The bottom line with principle number five is that you must take responsibility for embedding a system (keyword) into your business that generates a weekly flow of high-quality, inbound, new client inquiries. And furthermore you must stay in control of that flow or at the very least retain control of that flow inside of your business and not outside of it to a third party.

Outsourcing your lead generation to 3rd parties will fail on 9 out of 10 occasions because you'll just burn money and you'll get no leads, or all you'll get is very poor quality leads which will waste your time and frustrate you.

That does however leave the one out of 20 agencies that actually deliver results and from which you derive a significant return on your investment.

If you're fortunate enough to have found such an agency, please contact me and introduce me because I'll be the next one to sign up.

That said, I need to tell you why I would not hand over the bulk of my lead generation to even an agency that could generate a significant return on the fees that I would pay to them.

If I found a third-party agency that could generate very high quality new client inquiries then I would limit my exposure to them to a maximum of 30% of my new client inquiries volume because I would not want to create a dependency on that third party.

To do so would be the equivalent of outsourcing my entire oxygen supply for my body. I simply would be too vulnerable.

CHAPTER FOUR

The Three-part Inbound Marketing Model

In ORDER TO generate sales, as opposed to simply wasting money on "brand building," every effective marketing model, be that inbound or outbound, consists of three parts:

- An AUDIENCE
- An ASSET
- A call to ACTION

Clearly, we need someone to put our offer in front of. That someone is our Audience.

And we need a medium through which to make that offer, which our Asset.

Then we need to tell the Audience what to do if they want to move forward with us, and that is the call to Action.

To bring this to life, think about driving down the freeway, feeling hungry, and seeing a billboard offering drive-through food just next to the upcoming off-ramp.

In that scenario, you are the Audience, the billboard is the Asset, and the call to Action is inviting you to turn off the freeway and go get that meal.

Or a program handed out at a sports stadium where fans see an advertisement for the latest smart phone with a free calling number and free delivery. The Audience is the fans in the stadium, the Asset is the advertisement, and the call to Action is to dial the number and get the latest shiny thing.

In this chapter, I'll list examples for each of those three parts and in the following chapters I'll specify the very best option for each part and how they fit together, along with reasons why they represent your best option for generating a weekly flow of high-quality, inbound, new client inquiries.

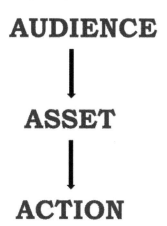

AUDIENCE Examples

Where do your ideal clients hang out?

The answer to that will yield a list of potential Audiences.

However, there is no point in listing all of your potential audiences because most of them will produce poor-quality leads and often for quite a lot of expenditure. With the following list I simply want to illustrate that it's easy to find Audiences. Later, I'll tell you where to find the best Audiences.

Here's just a relatively short list of possible Audiences.

1. Affiliate partners

2. Amazon book readers

3. Amusement park visitors

4. Blog subscribers

5. Bookstore shoppers

6. Bought or rented email or address lists

7. Business networking meetings

8. Clubs and associations

9. Conference attendees

10. Drivers and passengers

11. Facebook and Facebook Group members

12. Forums and message board contributors

13. Google search results

14. Google searchers

15. Joint Venture partners

16. Journal readers

17. LinkedIn and LinkedIn Groups

18. Mastermind Groups

19. Media lists of buyers and advertisers

20. Mobile phone APP users

21. Movie- and theater-goers

22. Newspaper and magazine readers (offline and online)

23. Online store shoppers

24. Other social media including Instagram and Twitter

25. Pay-Per-Click advertising

26. Personal observation

27. Press releases

28. Public relations

29. Radio and podcast listeners

30. Referrals - systemized

31. Referrals – word-of-mouth

32. Restaurants, cafes, drive-through patrons

33. Shopping mall shoppers

34. Sports stadiums attendees

35. Subscriber Email lists

36. Survey respondents

37. Television viewers

38. Tradeshow attendees

39. Visitors to transport hubs such as airports and train stations

40. Webinar attendees

41. Workshop and seminars attendees

42. YouTube viewers and subscribers

That list literally took me less than twelve minutes to put together. Hopefully, that reinforces my point, which is that finding Audiences is one of the easiest things in the world to do.

Finding the *right* Audience is a different matter because the source of your Audience is vital.

And once you have found the right Audience, then you must get the attention of that Audience and make them an offer via your Asset, in such a way that they take Action.

More on that in the next chapter, but in the meantime, let's look at the Asset part of our model.

ASSET EXAMPLES

An Asset is the Medium through which you get the Message about your Magic out to the Market.

(If you want more information about the Magic, Message, Medium and Market, please refer to my last book *Leadsology®: Marketing The Invisible.*

Like Audiences, you have myriad Asset options, which means that you have a lot of different options for getting your offer out to your ideal clients in a positive and added-value way.

In fact, this book is an Asset and therefore an example of how I'm getting the message about my magic out to you, my market.

That said, I wouldn't recommend that you write a book for your first Asset; there is a simpler, easier, faster, and more effective option that I'll reveal shortly.

But in the meantime, here is a list Assets that you *could* develop. Again, note that I'm not recommending that you develop all of these. They are simply offered by way of illustrating what I mean by a marketing Asset.

As you scan the list, you'll note that there is some repetition from the list of Audiences and that's because the whole point of a marketing Asset is to attract an Audience. That's why, for example, you'll see "Blog subscribers" in the Audience list and "Blog" in the Asset list.

1. Advertisements (online and offline)

2. APPs

3. Articles*

4. Audio book*

5. Billboard

6. Blog*

7. Blueprints

8. Books*

9. Boot Camp*

10. Brochure / Flyer

11. Cheat sheet

12. Diagnostic tool*

13. Direct mailer

14. E-books and e-guide*

15. Flowchart

16. Interactive guide*

17. Mini course or program*

18. Multi-day challenge*

19. Newsletter and e-letter

20. Online funnel

21. Podcast*

22. Quiz*

23. Retreat

24. Sample

25. Seminars and workshops

26. Social Media posts*

27. Speech or talk*

28. Survey*

29. Video

30. Webinars*

31. Websites including landing pages and sales pages*

32. YouTube channel

Once again, you have no shortage of options and, unlike the list of Audiences above, many of these Assets are effective enough to merit your consideration and I've placed an asterisk next to those that I personally utilize, be that for the purposes of direct lead generation or simply to keep "my brand in your brain until you are ready to buy."

It's important to note, however, that if I were starting again, there is only one Asset that I'd start with and that's the one I'll walk you through in great detail in Chapter Seven. It's also the Asset that after all my years in marketing, still consistently delivers more than 80% of my new client flows.

ACTION EXAMPLES

"Call To Action" (CTA) marketing or "Direct Response" marketing are one in the same thing. They both ask the Audience to do something that moves them closer to a purchase or indeed to make the purchase.

So, what's the best CTA for you as a professional advisor, service provider, planner or SaaS developer?

Here's a list of options for your consideration.

1. Answer

2. Ask

3. Attend

4. Buy

5. Call

6. Click

7. Connect

8. Download

9. Email

10. Engage

11. Enroll

12. Follow

13. Inquire

14. Interact

15. Invest

16. Join

17. Listen

18. Meet

19. Network

20. Post

21. Read

22. Re-blog

23. Recommend

24. Register

25. Re-tweet

26. Sample

27. Schedule

28. Share

29. Sponsorship

30. Subscribe or opt-in

31. Test

32. Trial

33. View

34. Write

In Chapter Eight, I'll reveal the best CTA and why it's the very best. And I'll not only reveal the component parts of the best CTA, but I'll let you know when to make your CTA, how to make it, and I'll also give you a real-life example that took me 11 years to perfect.

But for now, consider this: if you want to figure out how to generate leads, you have at least 42 types of Audiences, 32 types of Assets and 34 types of Actions to choose from. By using various combinations of those 108 components, you could end up with literally thousands of potential options for your marketing.

No wonder so many people are confused about where to start.

Some of my new clients tell me that, before they discovered my method, they felt like a deer trapped in the headlights of an oncoming truck, not knowing which way to turn because of the bright and shiny "lights" of so many different marketers telling them so many different ways to generate new clients.

And as discussed earlier, most of those recommendations are ineffective or expensive or complicated or take too long to yield results.

My method is superior because it's faster, simpler, easier, and more effective in generating a weekly flow of high-quality, inbound leads, than any other method I'm aware of or that I have tried and tested in the last 39 years as a professional marketer. Plus, once my method is up and running, you can operate it without any significant cost or complication.

Having said that, I'm aware that anyone can make claims like that.

But read on because I'm the one guy who puts his money where his mouth is: none of my program clients pay me even one cent upfront. I give them a full 30 days of complete access to every step of my three-part Audience, Asset, and Action system and I meet with them every week to help them implement that system and I give them an exclusive 24/7 messaging channel for questions and advice and I let them decide during those 30 days if I'm the real deal and if my model is right for them.

That's right: I give each new program client complete and full access to my intellectual property as well as all the support they need to implement, before I charge them anything.

That's my way of showing that I'm prepared to back my claims and let my clients decide if I'm right.

If you find anyone else who is prepared to back their system like I back my system, then put this book down and go ahead and work with them. You'll be in safe marketing hands.

Otherwise, I would like to suggest that it will be more profitable for you to read on.

CHAPTER FIVE

Your Best Inbound AUDIENCE

AUDIENCE

↓

ASSET

↓

ACTION

YOUR NUMBER ONE AUDIENCE CHOICE

AS A FULL-TIME professional in sales and marketing for 39 years, I've tried pretty much everything in terms of lead generation.

And remembering our context, which is marketing services advice and software where the average transaction numbers in the thousands or tens of thousands of dollars, (as opposed to physical products or inexpensive services and software), there is nothing that even comes close to generating both the quality and quantity of new client inquiries than Other Peoples Networks (OPN).

Also note that when I'm referring to Audiences, I'm doing so in the context of wanting to generate Audiences to attend my online meeting demonstration, which I'll cover in the next chapter.

To be more precise, the online meetings that I recommend that you host are where you demonstrate to Audience members how you work with your clients to achieve the sort of results that the attendees would also like to achieve.

So that's our context: you're offering advice services or software with the average transaction in thousands of dollars and you want an Audience for your online demonstration Asset.

That established, let's drill down and be more specific on what I mean by OPN which is **the email subscriber lists owned by other individuals who target the same market as you**.

It's important to note that I'm talking specifically about email subscriber lists where visitors to a website have opted in to an email list or have opted in indirectly by registering for some sort of event that the owner of that email subscriber list was running.

And in the interests of even more clarity, I am therefore not talking about email lists that were purchased or obtained through some other nefarious means.

I'm also not talking about social media connections including Facebook followers, Facebook Group members, LinkedIn connections, LinkedIn group members, Twitter followers, blog readers, podcast listeners or anyone else aside from individuals who have either directly or indirectly opted in to an email list as mentioned above.

OPN is a source of leads that is both of high-quality as well a significant volume (see Principle #5 above).

OPN is the undisputed champion when we apply the criteria of quality and quantity in the context of marketing professional advice services or software where the average transaction sale is in the thousands or tens of thousands or even hundreds of thousands of dollars.

Nothing else even comes close.

You can take my word for this or you can spend the decades in the marketing wilderness and waste those years together with hundreds of thousands of dollars, like I did, trying everything else under the sun.

My guess is that because you have purchased this book and because, even more importantly, you've read this far, you're going to be the sort of person who tends to recognize the voice of experience when you hear it.

So good for you.

But having acknowledged your likely astuteness, it's still important that you never take anyone's word simply on face value. Including mine.

Every marketer must be able to explain their advice to you in clear, rational, and logical terms so that you're able to understand why they are making those recommendations in such a way that you can reasonably conclude that their advice is sound.

If you feel like a marketing advisor is using "smoke and mirrors" and is being vague or hyping things up, then run away fast.

With that in mind, let me expand on why other people's email lists are your number one best source of high-quality new client inquiries.

First though, I'll briefly answer a question I get a lot at this point, which is why I don't simply refer to OPN as a Joint Venture.

And the answer is that I call it something different because it is something different.

I've continually developed the OPN concept since 1995 and I've refined it to the point where it is different from the traditional Joint Venture arrangement. It's like the difference between a website and a mobile phone APP. The latter may have developed from the former but it's being refined so much that they are most definitely completely separate categories of software.

The other reason is that the term Joint Venture can mean a lot of different things to a lot of different people, but with OPN, I get to define exactly what I mean so that you, my valued reader, are crystal clear about where the gold is and how to get into the goldmine.

WHY OPN IS THE BEST SOURCE OF LEADS

When you look at the myriad options you have for getting your marketing message in front of an Audience (see the previous chapter), almost all of them are expensive or complicated or difficult or unsustainable or they take too long to work, or they are ineffective.

But if you take the opposite of those six characteristics (expensive, complicated, difficult, unsustainable, takes too long, ineffective) what you get is :

- Inexpensive
- Simpler
- Easier
- Sustainable
- Faster
- Effective

And that's the exact six characteristics that are embodied in OPN.

Our course everything is relative so, for example, when I say "inexpensive" I naturally mean that it's expensive relative to other options. Ditto for the other characteristics.

But let me briefly explain each of those six characteristics so that you are crystal clear as to why OPN is the marketing goldmine that you've been seeking.

Inexpensive

There are no advertising costs or affiliate fees, or any other direct acquisition fees associated with OPN.

For all intents and purposes, it is a source of high-quality leads that's completely free of any direct acquisition costs.

Virtually every single month I have OPN Partners who happily send out email invitations (that I've written and provided) to their email list inviting their subscribers to attend one of my online lead-generation demonstrations.

In most cases, these OPN Partners did not know me from a bar of soap a month or two prior to promoting my event.

And in every case, they have promoted my event without me paying them one cent in commissions or fees of any description.

The question that probably comes to your mind right now, is why on earth would someone promote my online demonstration without me paying them any money and without them having any longstanding knowledge of me, my products or services, or my brand?

Great question and I'll answer it shortly.

But in the meantime, just know that you don't have to spend any money on advertising or affiliate fees or other direct acquisition costs in order to generate a predictable flow of high-quality, inbound, new client inquiries.

I'm aware that we normally associate something that's more expensive with something that's better quality, but when it comes to marketing advice services or software, and the source of new clients, the exact opposite applies.

Simpler, faster and easier

To answer the above question of why someone would promote my online presentation is that, when I source my prospects from other people's email lists, there is a very simple value exchange which takes place that normally involves some form of cross-marketing to each other's email lists.

And before you email me to tell me that you don't have an email list or that you have a very small email list, let me assure you that everyone starts with no list or a small list.

But you start, and you work your way up.

With my method, as you engage in cross-marketing campaigns with the right OPN partners, you build your email list with each campaign, and you spiral up to other OPN partners with larger email lists though cross referral from one OPN Partner to new OPN Partners after you complete each campaign.

That established, when you compare cross-marketing an offer from one email list to another, there really is no other form of effective marketing that is as simple and as easy and that gets results as fast. For example:

- Online funnels are massively more complicated.

- It takes longer to set up a freeway billboard and it's more expensive and less effective.

- Radio advertisements are more difficult and are expensive and less effective.

- Posting to LinkedIn is over 99% less effective and incredibly time-consuming.

I could go on, but if you've read Chapter Three, you are most likely up to speed with this, so I won't belabor the point by going on and on about less-effective sources of Audiences.

Sustainable

I've yet to find a client who doesn't have hundreds of OPN partner opportunities.

More often, those opportunities number in the thousands or the tens of thousands or the hundreds of thousands.

It's absolutely mind-boggling how many OPN opportunities exist in the United States alone.

Provided you're prepared to reach out and deliver value to clients beyond the geographical region that you can easily access by car, then the number of OPN partner opportunities are such that you will never fish that particular pond dry.

OPN is a method that I have employed week after week, month after month, year after year and decade after decade, and one that shows absolutely no sign of becoming exhausted.

In fact, exactly the opposite is true: as established economies grow and as new economies are established and as the digital reach of the Internet expands, the opportunities for OPN partnerships is impossible to keep up with.

WHO MAKES THE BEST OPN PARTNER?

I've kept track of OPN partners since 1995.

And I've refined my checklist of who makes the best OPN partners ever since then.

I have, in fact, gone a lot further in this area than any of my contemporaries that I'm aware of by hiring two highly qualified data scientists to analyze all of my OPN partnerships from a purely mathematical perspective, and I've combined their findings along with my own subjective observations as to who makes the best OPN partners.

It goes without saying that the first characteristic of an OPN partner is that **they must have an email subscriber list** that's attracting opt ins from people who would represent your ideal client.

Of course, this is not to say that every single person who opts in to an OPN partner's email list is going to be an ideal client.

You need to reference my metaphor of the 100 Sleeping Bears in Chapter One to understand that there is no way of telling which email subscribers are my ideal clients until after I put the "honey pot outside the forest."

However, it's very easy to tell if someone has an email subscriber list: you simply go to their website and see if they have something valuable on offer in exchange for a visitor's email address.

The second characteristic I look for in an OPN partner is that they **feature themselves prominently on their website**.

Again, it's very easy to validate this characteristic. Simply visit their website and see if they have a photo of themselves and an "about" page. Someone who doesn't feature themselves on the website will not make a great OPN partner for you.

The reason is simple. Small-business marketing works differently than big-business marketing. The latter can rely on creating a relationship with their brand, such as Coca-Cola or McDonald's. They can spend millions of dollars establishing a relationship of trust with their audiences.

Small businesses can't afford to do that. We simply don't have the budget of a big business.

But while the lack of a multimillion-dollar budget might seem to be a disadvantage, it is in fact an advantage because you have something that no corporate giant can offer, which is your personality. People follow big brands, or they follow personalities, or in rare cases such as Elon Musk or Richard Branson they may follow both.

The bottom line with this second OPN Partner characteristic is that you're looking for someone who has established a relationship of trust between their personality and their email subscribers.

Without that trust, a potential OPN partner, even with a large email list, won't have the necessary level of influence with their subscribers for the latter to follow the recommendation of that OPN partner and thereby register for the online demonstration (see the next chapter on ASSET) that I recommend you host.

The third characteristic that I'm looking for in a potential OPN partner is that **they target the same target market as me**. This one doesn't really take much explaining: I'm looking for that forest of 100 Sleeping Bears.

So, if you're a business coach, you're looking for people who have email lists targeting small business owners.

And if you're an executive coach, then you're looking for people who have email lists targeting executive coaches.

And if you're a financial planner, then you're probably looking for people who have email lists that are targeting pre-retirees.

And if you're a management consultant, then you're looking for people who have built email lists that are targeting organizations of a similar size and with similar needs to your own target market.

Once again, this is very easy to validate because you can simply visit their website and their LinkedIn profile, which are the two main places people will go when they want to check someone out.

The fourth characteristic is to make sure that **they are assertively marketing themselves** through webinars or via pay-per-click advertising or blog posts or podcasts or a bestselling book on Amazon or preferably a multiple of the above options. In other words, they must be assertively, if not aggressively, marketing themselves.

A simple Google search of their name will confirm the extent of their marketing activity levels.

Anyone who is not active on the world wide web looking for new clients is not going to be open to an OPN partnership.

Remember: effective marketing places an offer in front of someone who is already looking for that offer.

Never waste your time attempting to convince someone that the strategy that you're offering is the right one for them.

You are better off spending a fraction of the time you would waste in "convincing" someone to find someone who is already looking for a way to execute strategy that you can provide them with.

That's what smart marketing does: if puts an offer in front of someone who is looking for that offer.

The fifth characteristic that you need to confirm is that **they offer the same category of service as you.**

For example if you're offering some form of professional development, then you need to find people who are doing the same.

OPN partnerships never work when one party offers a professional development service and the other is a personal development service. If you fall into the latter category, then you're looking for OPN partners who also offer some form of personal development service.

By way of extension of that, the sixth characteristic is that **they are offering services advice or software and not a physical product**.

If you're one of my ideal clients, then you're offering services advice or software and an OPN partnership with someone who has an otherwise great email list but who offers physical products, will never work for me.

By way of example, 24 years ago when I was still figuring this stuff out, I set up an OPN campaign with the country's largest supplier of computer hardware to small business.

They had a massive email list, but the campaign resulted in precisely zero new clients for me.

Subscribers to an email list of someone who sells physical products will not listen to their recommendations when it comes to non-physical services.

The seventh characteristic that I look for runs completely contrary to the traditionally recommended Joint Venture method, which is that you seek out someone who offers a complementary service to the same target market as you.

The theory is that you should avoid people who offer something similar to you because your prospective JV partner will not want to cross market with you because you are targeting the same market with similar offerings.

For example, the aforementioned traditional approach to a joint venture campaign would match a corporate sales trainer with the human resource consultant because they both target the same market but with services that are not competing against each other.

This was what I also believed for far too many years before I discovered that my most successful OPN partnerships were with people who were offering lead generation training, advice, software, programs, seminars, workshops, masterminds and so on. In other words, they are offering something that is either the same or very similar to what I'm offering.

The seventh characteristic that I look for is therefore **someone who is as close as possible to offering what I offer,** which is of course lead generation.

The reason that these people make the best OPN partners is because their email subscribers have opted in to that person's email list and by doing so have registered a direct interest in lead generation, which happens to be a need that I can also meet.

It's logical that a prospect who opted in to someone else's email subscriber list which offers marketing content, and then registers for my webinar where I demonstrate how I work with my clients to generate leads, is going to be a high-quality prospect. They've moved through two filters, flagging their interest in what I offer.

But that leaves us with the question as to why someone who many in the marketplace would perceive to be my direct competitor would want to promote their competitor: i.e. me.

The reason is that mature marketers understand that there are some people on their email subscriber list who will never actually buy from them, but who may buy from me.

And the reverse also applies.

There are people on my email list who might like the idea of lead generation but for some reason don't click with my style, which is very prescriptive. But they might click with the style of an OPN partner who is more conceptual or high level.

The bottom line with the seventh characteristic is that if I can find someone who is a mature marketer, with a large email list and who has established a relationship of trust with that list, then they will make the very best OPN partner.

So, when you're looking for OPN partners, don't leave money on the table by assuming that someone who might be perceived to be a direct competitor will not promote your services.

In my experience, over 80% of mature marketers ("mature" being the operative word), will happily enter into some form of cross-marketing campaign with a direct competitor.

It's true that the balance will not. And I respect their right to choose a more exclusive strategy whereby they never position themselves in such a way that they are seen to endorse a competitor.

Personally, I think it's a very shortsighted strategy and I suspect that is motivated out of a false sense of scarcity or professional insecurity. But, that's their call and, fortunately for me, there are plenty of other fish in the OPN sea.

How to Approach an OPN Prospect

Now that you're equipped with the seven characteristics of an ideal OPN partner, you'll appreciate that identifying the right people has suddenly become relatively easy and certainly infinitely more profitable.

But there is a massive gulf between identifying an OPN partner and establishing a relationship with them of Rapport, Respect, Relatability and Reciprocity.

These are what I call the "Four Rs of Psychological Allure" and I covered them adequately in my last book *Leadsology®: Marketing The Invisible* so I won't go into any detail again here.

But for those readers who may not have read that book, let me just say that you need a whole lot more than Rapport with a prospective OPN partner before that will voluntarily promote you.

The establishment of a trusted relationship with prospective OPN partner starts with the approach.

And that approach cannot be about what you want.

I know I've said this before, but I really cannot say it often enough: effective marketing makes someone an offer that they are already looking for.

If you approach someone who you have correctly identified as a potentially effective OPN partner with what you want, you will probably not receive the courtesy of a response, let alone a positive response.

You'll recall that we are looking for people who are already marketing their services assertively, if not aggressively.

So, you know that they are looking for an opportunity to promote themselves and their services.

Your approach must therefore be to make them an offer that allows them to promote themselves.

You can do that by offering to repost their blog or the article they posted to LinkedIn or by having them on your podcast or by retweeting their tweets or any other way that takes something they are already marketing and offering to share that with your social media connections and your email list, be that large or small.

With no strings attached.

WHEN TO BRIDGE FROM OPN PROSPECT TO OPN PARTNER

There is a litmus test that you can use to indicate when it's the right time to bridge from having identified someone as a prospective OPN partner and when to approach them about a cross-marketing campaign.

The litmus test is this: if you called them on their mobile phone and they could see that it was you who was calling, and assuming they weren't in a meeting or otherwise occupied, would they pick up the phone and greet you by your first name?

If they would, then it's time to set up a meeting with them and talk about a cross-marketing campaign.

(Note that this exercise is only conducted in your imagination because chances are you won't have their mobile phone number.)

But if you believe that they would let your call go through to voicemail or worse, that they wouldn't even know who you were despite your name showing up on their screen, then you have not yet earned the right to bring up the subject of a cross-marketing campaign.

That's when you go back to their LinkedIn profile and back to their website and back to Google searching their name and finding out what it is they want to market and offering to help them with that.

Go ahead and look up the definition of "reciprocity."

It is the most underrated and least talked about, and yet the most heavy-duty influencer in the psychology of marketing.

Use reciprocity ethically and with positive intent to help as many people as you can and you will become the living personification of the person who "cast their bread upon the water" to have it returned to them, as a triple layered chocolate sponge cake.

You can become very wealthy by the simple act of helping people get what they want.

THE THREE OPN PARTNER ARCHETYPES AND THEIR PRIMARY MOTIVATION FOR PARTNERING WITH YOU

I'm in love with marketing.

And I'm also in love with scaling a business so that results, including revenue, increase in a way that is completely disproportionate to the resources being devoted to stimulating those increases.

And because of those twin loves, I'm fascinated by the leverage that segmentation provides.

I touch on this in my book *Leadsology®: The Science Of Being In Demand* and also in my book *The Million-Dollar Ceiling*. But again, assuming that you haven't read either of those books, let me just say that segmentation is all about breaking down a long and more complex process into a series of small parts.

In his book *The Wealth of Nations*, Adam Smith outlined the concept of segmentation in the example of a factory manufacturing pins. Henry Ford revolutionized the manufacturing of vehicles, and manufacturing in general, by applying the principles of segmentation when he created the modern world's first manufacturing assembly line.

Segmentation not only provides you with the potential for *scalability* but also empowers you with the capability of *specialization*.

When you segment your marketplace, then you create the opportunity to develop specialized information and skills to serve that marketplace.

A case in point is that I specialize with professionals who offer services advice or software whose average transaction can be measured by thousands of dollars. By segmenting my whole potential market and specializing only in this restricted sub-market, I dramatically increase both the effectiveness of my marketing as well as the effectiveness of my solutions.

All of which brings me to the point of this section, which is that not all OPN partners are created equal.

In broad terms, we can segment your potential OPN partners into three categories, which are Merchants, Missionaries, and Mercenaries.

Each of these three OPN segments can be a goldmine for you provided you understand that they each have a different motivation.

The Merchant

In the context of OPN, I'm referring to The Merchant as a trader who trades one set of goods for another. The classic OPN scenario that I described above in the section where I identified an ideal OPN Partner's seven characteristics, describes The Merchant quite adequately.

The Merchant is motivated primarily by reciprocity.

You promote their stuff and they promote your stuff.

No money changes hands; you are simply trading one set of goods for another set of goods. In the case of The Merchant, the goods that you are trading are respective exposures to each other's email lists.

You can trade in the form of a podcast swap, a webinar swap, a blog promotion swap, a free gift swap or anything else that you each have that represents value for the other's email list.

The Missionary

Maslow's famous Hierarchy of Needs teaches us that once we feel secure that our survival needs such as food and shelter have been met, then we feel more motivated to improve our lifestyle, and once those Lifestyle needs have been met, then we move on to being motivated by more altruistic needs such as helping others.

Someone who is struggling to put food on the table for their family in an impoverished third world country is not going to be focused on saving the world from climate change.

Likewise, someone who is at the top of their business game and who has achieved mastery and made tens of millions of dollars is going to be far more concerned about providing value to their email subscribers than they will be about reciprocity like The Merchant is.

I'm not saying that The Missionary is not going to be unconcerned about reciprocity, but rather that they are going to be less concerned about that, as opposed to making a positive difference in the lives of their email subscribers, which is why I refer to them, metaphorically speaking, as The Missionary.

The Missionary has a different motivation than The Merchant. And while comparing them to Mother Theresa would most definitely be a stretch, they are equally most definitely more motivated by making a difference than they are by making money than The Merchant or The Mercenary (see below).

In the world of marketing, The Missionary is a rare beast indeed. And they are also quite hard to identify until you get to know them personally and understand how much of their time and money they commit to philanthropy and how they genuinely care about helping the people who are their team members, clients, suppliers, and prospects.

But they do exist and while I'm not recommending that you target them specifically, neither should you assume that someone with a much larger email list would not consider promoting an offer of yours, provided that your offer was both interesting and valuable to their email subscribers.

The Mercenary

Every metaphor or analogy can be stretched too far, and such is the case with my use of the term "Mercenary."

However, if you're impatient and you have a small email list, then this is definitely the OPN segment that you should consider as a priority.

Once you've created a world-class marketing Asset (see Chapter Six) and you have proved you can generate clients with that Asset (see Chapter Seven), then you can rapidly accelerate your email list building and new client generating, by working with The Mercenary.

I am aware that the average Mercenary is not generally viewed in a favorable light by the general public. They are people who kill for money. They are like hitmen or hitwomen who join together in a group to form a private army for hire.

In the context of OPN however, The Mercenary only has one thing in common with the above-mentioned private army, which is that they are very motivated by money and therefore less motivated by reciprocation (like The Merchant) or making the world a better place (like The Missionary).

So, if you have a small email list, then offering The Mercenary an affiliate commission is a valid and viable strategy. Otherwise, stick to The Merchants and The Missionaries or adopt the next idea, quickly.

THE FASTEST AND SIMPLEST WAY TO ESTABLISH AND GROW A QUALITY EMAIL LIST

When a new client of mine explains to me that they don't have an email list, or they have a very small email list. I tell them that "we were all born naked."

None of us was born with an email list so the best thing to do is to start developing one. Right away.

If you don't already have an online email database, then you can start today, by signing up for one of the many free versions such as www.mailchimp.com and populate it with everyone who has shared their email address with you in the past in the context of your current business.

It really doesn't matter whether you have one person or 100 people or 1,000 people ready to populate your online email database.

The important thing is to start.

To paraphrase Goethe: the magic, genius, and power is beginning a thing and the moment you commit to a certain endeavor, all sort of things, previously unforeseen, start to occur to help you in that undertaking.

You should of course set up what is referred to as "a lead magnet" in the form of an offer on your website where people can opt in. If you go to my website at www.leadsology.guru, you'll find plenty of examples.

But that doesn't help you much if you've got no traffic going to your website.

So, while you should definitely have something to offer on your website that visitors can opt in to receive in exchange for the email address, and have those opt-ins populate your new email database (see above), you'll also need a method of growing your email list that doesn't initially rely on significant volumes of website traffic.

The simplest and easiest and fastest way to establish a quality email list is to set up and host a webinar panel where you have three specialist panelists who each target your target market and who possess the seven characteristics that I featured above in the section of how to identify an ideal OPN partner.

Each of the three specialists will therefore have a high-quality email list and they will promote the webinar to their list via an email that you're provide them with, which will include the link for those email subscribers to register for the webinar panel.

In your capacity as the host and facilitator of the webinar panel, you let people know on the webinar registration page that, in registering for the webinar, they will also be opting into the email subscriber lists of each of your panelists as well as your own email list.

You'll assure them equally as explicitly that the contact details will not be shared with anyone else and that they'll be able to unsubscribe easily and simply at any time by using the link at the bottom of any emails they receive.

(All online email database platforms provide an unsubscribe link at the bottom of each mini email that you send out.)

THE SPIRAL: HOW TO RACHET UP THE QUALITY OF YOUR OPN PARTNERS EVERY 90 DAYS

Most months, I conduct four cross-marketing campaigns with OPN partners.

Those people mistakenly believe that these cross-marketing campaigns is where I make most of my money.

And while it's true that 80% of my new client revenue is derived from such campaigns, most of the money is made *after* the campaigns.

It would be easy to make the mistake of thinking that the purpose of securing an OPN partner is to conduct a cross-marketing campaign, but in fact it's completely the opposite: the purpose of conducting a cross-marketing campaign is to secure an OPN partner.

To clarify, there's a lot more money to be made from your relationship with an effective OPN partner then there is to be made from any one-off cross-marketing campaign.

And this is where almost all my colleagues who conduct some form of Joint Venture or cross-marketing exercises leave significant amounts of money on the table, so to speak.

With my method, after the completion of each campaign I digitally sit down with my OPN partner and conduct a debrief to firstly confirm that the campaign was mutually beneficial.

If for some reason, it's turned out that I've been deficient in reciprocating, then I offer to make it up by promoting something else for them.

Often however, both partners are satisfied with the outcome because I've been careful prior to approaching and engaging with that OPN partner to establish that they were likely to be able to reciprocate at a similar level.

That said, once were I've confirmed that my OPN partner was happy with the outcome, I'll then move on to initiate the process of referring them to three other OPN partners who were able to reciprocate at a similar level to them.

And they will do the same in return.

As I complete these debriefs, I am typically referred to 3 different levels of prospective future OPN partners.

There are those who will not be able to reciprocate at the same level and there are those who will be able to reciprocate at a similar level and there will be those who reciprocate at a much higher level.

And by "level" I'm referring to the results that each partner is able to generate for the other, be that new email subscribers or webinar attendees or podcast listeners or whatever form a cross-marketing campaign has taken.

What this means over any given 90 day period is that I've been referred to over 30 prospective new OPN partners and on the law of averages 10 of those are going to represent a smaller opportunity than the past OPN partner who referred me, 10 will represent a similar opportunity, and 10 will represent a bigger opportunity.

For example, an OPN partner that I completed a webinar swap with may have generated say 100 webinar registrants for my webinar.

When that partner refers me to three other prospective OPN partners, then one of them may be capable of generating 50 webinar registrants and another may be capable of generating 100 and the third one may be capable of generating 200 or more webinar registrants.

Of course, I'm talking about the law of averages. It never works out exactly that way with any one set of OPN partner referrals. Over a 90-day period however, it does work out pretty much that way.

That means that every 90 days, I spiral up the OPN "food chain" so to speak, into an ever-improving and ever-larger network of potential ideal clients.

Now back to you: you might start cross-marketing with OPN partners who have a dozen or more subscribers on the email list.

Or you might start cross-marketing with OPN partners who have hundreds or thousands of email subscribers. It really is not important where you start; it's important that you do start.

And from there you spiral up.

And up.

And up.

Provided you follow my system, you're systematical and continual enjoyment of greater success in lead generation is absolutely and unequivocally assured.

Other Valid Audience Options

AUDIENCE

ASSET

ACTION

As you know, my marketing model consists of the Audience, the Asset and the call to Action.

I've written about why OPN is your very best source for your Audiences and in the next chapter I'll explain why the online demonstration is your very best Asset.

But first I want to point you in the direction of other sources of leads that can, in certain circumstances, also be highly profitable *after* you've started to mine the gold in the OPN gold mine.

LinkedIn

In chapter 2, I ran into detail on why LinkedIn doesn't work as a lead generator for Audiences the way most people think that works, which is by nurturing and slowing building brand awareness.

Nevertheless, for me LinkedIn is a high-quality source of Audiences that supplements my OPN source and it generates new clients for me like clockwork, pretty much every month of the year without me even logging in to my LinkedIn account.

By using third-party specialist LinkedIn contractors and having them connect with my ideal clients via their own LinkedIn account, and having those connections then be invited to attend my online lead generation demonstration, I establish a low-quantity but a high-quality additional stream of new client inquiries.

You might want to read that again to make sure you read it right: I wrote "low quantity."

In my experience, LinkedIn is best at producing a lower number of inquiries from people who are more likely to spend a lot more with me than those who are from other sources.

And that's why I steer some of my new clients in the direction of my program that adds LinkedIn as a source of audiences in addition to OPN.

Typically, those new clients include management consultants, corporate trainers, and executive coaches, along with financial planners. Each of these client categories tends to need a lower number of clients whose average transaction size is a lot larger than those of my other clients. And LinkedIn is perfect for that.

Search Engine Optimization (SEO)

SEO is where you figure out what your ideal clients are searching for online and making sure that your website is featured near the top of organic search results in Google. And by "organic," that contrasts with paid search results, which is also commonly referred to as Pay Per Click or PPC.

SEO can work very well as an additional source of Audiences but requires a longer-term commitment and a small team of content writers to make it work.

So, it's not the place that I recommend you start at.

OPN is that place and LinkedIn is the next best place so don't contemplate SEO until you have ticked the others to implement first.

CHAPTER SIX

Your Best Inbound ASSET

YOUR NUMBER ONE **ASSET** CHOICE

IN CHAPTER TWO and Chapter Four, I listed a lot of different Assets by which you can get the message about your magic out to the market.

And by highlighting your very best option, I'm not for a moment suggesting that it is your only option.

But as stated earlier, my intention is to give you your very best option for implementing your very first lead generation system that will predictably bring in a weekly flow of high-quality, inbound, new client inquiries.

Having acknowledged that, I can categorically assure you that your very best choice, from literally more than 100 options, is to use online presentations as the Asset through which to get your message and offer out to your market.

Online presentations give you the maximum beneficial combination of efficiency and effectiveness. And it's the combination of those two sets of benefits that is important.

There are more efficient ways to get your message out to the market, but they are **not as effective**.

For example, radio or television advertising. You can simply pick up the phone and order some advertisements and the agency will do everything for you. But they won't be effective for the reasons outlined in Chapter Three: The Five Principles of Effective Inbound Marketing.

And there are more effective ways to get your message out to the market, but they are **not as efficient**.

For example, I can hire a conference center, run a bunch of advertisements and speak to centers of influence, and pack as many people into a conference room as possible.

I can then present to that Audience for anywhere between a couple of hours and a couple of days and because I'll be in the room physically with the attendees, I'll be able to establish higher levels of Rapport, Respect, Relatability and Reciprocity than I could with a one-hour online meeting.

But that's a massively more complicated (and expensive) way of getting my message out to the market. Trust me on this, I've conducted over 500 such events.

In summary, in terms of the combination of efficiency and effectiveness, online presentation beats every other single method for generating inquiries.

Online presentations are commonly referred to as webinars, which of course is derived from the word seminar but differentiated to denote that the seminar is being delivered over the World Wide Web.

I stumbled upon the webinar concept in 2007 soon after Citrix launched GoToWebinar and I was one of their early adopters. As alluded to above, I had spent the previous 12 years speaking at over 500 conference events internationally and I was getting a little tired of the travelling and the hotel rooms.

To me, it was bordering on the miraculous that I could present the same information from my seminars in a webinar, and that my commute would suddenly switch from driving my car or flying in a plane, to the 30 yards that I walked from the espresso machine in my kitchen to my office at the other end of our home.

Most people refer to online meetings as webinars, but I don't because I want to make the distinction between the traditional webinar which is typically attended by dozens or hundreds or even thousands of people, and a derivative of that which I'll introduce you to shortly.

The reason for making the distinction is because, as mentioned in the previous chapter, making distinctions through segmentation is the key to improving your results. More on that soon.

WHY AN ONLINE PRESENTATION IS YOUR BEST OPTION FOR GENERATING INBOUND LEADS

I mentioned above that online presentations offer the best combination of efficiency and effectiveness for generating high-quality inbound inquiries.

Now I want to dive down and give you more specific reasons to back up that claim.

Here are ten reasons why online presentations are your best option for your marketing Asset:

1. With online meetings you get to avoid Hugh Jackman Marketing

In chapter 3, I explained why marketing services and advice and software for transactions that are measured in thousands or tens of thousands of dollars is more like proposing marriage than it is selling, say, a washing machine.

Online meetings give you enough time to establish The Four Rs of Psychological Allure that I mentioned previously being Rapport, Respect, Relatability and Reciprocity.

If you are going to convince an understandably skeptical audience as to why they should hand over a big chunk of money to you, then you absolutely must establish those four levels of psychological allure. You simply can't do that on a billboard or with a 30-second radio commercial.

2. With online meetings you get to do what you want to do and not what you feel you should do

Just yesterday, I met with one of my Advisory Board members, Thomas Kessler, who lives in Bonn, Germany.

Thomas's background is as a merger and acquisitions consultant and he has worked with some of the biggest consultancy firms in the world, consulting on countless large and complicated regional and global mergers and acquisitions.

Needless to say, I do not share his capacity to make sense out of complexity. Metaphorically speaking, he's the cat to my dog (see Principle Number Two in Chapter Three).

Thomas and I were meeting one-on-one, online, preparing for an upcoming board meeting.

The purpose of our meeting was to make sure that we had the answers to the financial questions that the other board members might throw at us.

Thomas spent 15 minutes explaining to me different options for financial modelling, cash flow forecasting, and the difference between profit and EBITA (Google it if you dare).

This is what I said to him when he finished: "Thomas you've just spent 15 minutes telling a fish how to climb a tree."

He blinked a couple of times and then started to chuckle.

I probably could have said that he just spent 15 minutes trying to teach a dog how to meow.

It would have turned out to be just as futile because I really didn't understand what he was talking about and I suspect that, even if I had understood, I'd fail to see the relevance to achieving the revenue objectives that my Advisory Board is charged with achieving.

What's the bottom line?

It is that all of us have brains that work differently and that different brains are inclined to want to do different things.

One person's "want to" is another person's "should do."

On the subject of "want to," my strong suspicion is that if you woke up tomorrow morning and checked your calendar, and saw that there were more than 100 interested prospects registered for an online presentation where you would share about how you work with your clients, that your brain would "want to" attend that meeting.

There are a couple of provisos in that scenario.

The first is that you have a presentation prepared (your Asset) that you enjoy presenting and that you are confident in presenting and that you know will receive the appreciation of all attendees regardless of whether they become clients or not.

Another proviso is that you know from experience that your presentation is likely to generate a number of bookings in your calendar for the upcoming week, from highly qualified prospects who want to talk with you and confirm that working with you is the right thing to do.

So, am I right?

If that scenario played out tomorrow morning, would you want to attend and present?

If the answer is yes, then you should keep reading because I'm going to show you how to create an Asset (your online presentation) so that you enjoy presenting it and also that it is extraordinarily effective in both educating your Audience as well is qualifying them to ensure they are a good fit for working with you, as well as motivating them to take Action (see Chapter Seven) by booking a time to talk with you about becoming a client.

If the answer is no, that you would not want to present to that group of 100 well-qualified and motivated prospects, even though you have a brilliant presentation that adds great value to attendees and that you enjoy delivering, then you should definitely assign this book to the nearest rubbish bin, digital or otherwise.

3. Online meetings give you the volume that you need

For you to enjoy a systematically predictable weekly flow of high-quality, inbound, new client inquiries, you must have volume.

High volume covers a multitude of deficiencies.

By way of explanation, consider the following:

If I have one of the best presentations in the world and no one attends it, I'm not going to generate any new client inquiries.

By contrast, if I have one of the worst presentations in the world but I have one billion people attending, I'm going to have more new client inquiries than I could possibly handle.

I'll be the first to put my hand up and say that if I had to choose between quality and quantity, I would prioritize the former over the latter.

But you don't have to choose.

You can have both.

An online presentation allows you get your message and offer out to a large number of people, very efficiently and very effectively.

4. Online meetings give you an effective filter to improve the quality of your inquiries

Not all marketing Assets are created equal.

Not all marketing Assets deliver the same quantity and quality of prospects.

By way of example, I will generate comparatively fewer email subscribers from this book than I will by offering a free gift to the subscribers of one of my OPN partners.

But the clients that are generated from the subscribers that were sourced from this book, will on average pay *eight times* more to work with me than someone who became a client after subscribing via the free gift offer.

The reason for that is that someone who is prepared to read my book, and then become an email subscriber, is far more motivated than someone who opts in as an email subscriber in exchange for a free gift.

Firstly, my book reader has paid money whereas the free gift email subscriber has not.

Secondly, my book reader has put time and effort into reading my book whereas the free gift email subscriber may have simply downloaded the free gift and never looked at it.

And thirdly, we know from multiple surveys, that the readers of books are likely to be better educated and have more money than nonreaders.

I'm providing those two extreme examples to illustrate the point that the source of your prospects is a key determinant both of their likelihood to make an inquiry about your services as well as their capacity to pay premium fees.

Attendees to online meetings fit somewhere in between the two extremes illustrated above.

They haven't had to pay any money.

(I've tested this extensively and there is really very little point in charging for attendance.)

But they did have to attend the meeting and stick around to the end, which is where you tell them what they need to do if they want to inquire about working with you.

More on that the next chapter.

To put this another way, they put *some* skin in the game.

They made a commitment.

While they may not have invested money, they have invested their time, which I would argue is more valuable than their money because time is a finite resource whereas money is virtually infinite.

By reason of the law of supply and demand, time is therefore worth more than money. Many a wealthy dying person would have given away everything in order to live for another 10 years.

The attendee of your online presentation is a high-quality prospect compared to others who subscribe via almost all of the other types of lead generation Assets.

5. Online meetings combined with my OPN method has you in charge of the leads supply

I've covered this adequately in Principle Number Five In Chapter Three: for the sake of your security and prosperity, you must retain responsibility for, and control of, lead generation for your business.

By combining my OPN system with online presentations, you achieve exactly that.

6. Online meetings are both time- and cost-efficient

I mentioned the fact that when presenting an online meeting my commute is from the espresso machine in my kitchen down the hallway to my home office. You can't get much more time efficient than that.

In terms of costs, www.zoom.us will provide you with a free webinar platform for up to 100 participants and for up to 40 minutes. Most of my clients don't need greater capacity than 100 attendees.

Also, note that most webinar platforms allow you to register double the amount of people than they give you capacity for attendees.

In other words, a platform that gives you the capacity for 100 attendees will likely provide you with the capacity for up to 200 registrants, because they know that less than half of the registrants will turn up to your meeting.

And if you want to splash out a little more and pay $15 - $30 a month, then you can run meetings of an hour or more and have literally hundreds of attendees, depending on the platform you choose.

I cover some of your platform options later, but for now let me just state the obvious, which is that running online meetings is extraordinarily time- and cost-efficient.

7. Online meetings give you global reach

Our house sits on golden sand next to the deep blue sea and white waves at little castaways Beach in Queensland, Australia.

We are surrounded by a park full of birds, bees, and trees. My wife and I go to sleep to the sound of waves and wake up to the sound of birdsong.

It's as close to paradise as I've ever seen.

And yet, once a month when I run my online presentations, I reach out from our little slice of heaven to attendees right across the world.

I typically run two webinars, once a month. The first one I run at 4 p.m. Eastern USA time and the second one I run at 3 a.m. Eastern USA which, outside of daylight savings, will be 8 a.m. in London and 5 p.m. in Sydney, Australia.

For someone who was born before the Internet, and who spent many years having to commute to conference centers via car or planes in order to address Audiences full of my ideal clients, the instantaneous reach of online presentations is miraculous.

With online presentations you can reach out to the people in the building next door to you or to Audiences on the other side of the world.

I would urge you to commit to the strategy of making online presentations your number one priority.

And for those of you, my valued readers, who are tempted to discount the validity and efficacy of online presentations because "my clients are simply too busy to attend an online meeting," let me assure you that you would be making a grave mistake to believe such a mistruth.

If you have what your ideal client wants, they will crawl over broken glass to get it.

My clients who serve the busiest, most time poor and most stressed market in the world, which are the senior executives of some of the world's biggest organizations, have proved the lie to the idea that busy people will not attend an online meeting.

They will attend, but you may have to up your game in terms of how you articulate the benefit for attendees.

If you build it, they will come.

8. With online meetings the sources of your leads are 100% trackable

One of the most well-known quotes in advertising circles is credited to John Wanamaker who said: "half the money I spend on advertising is wasted; the trouble is I don't know which half."

By contrast, when you set up a registration page for prospects to register for your online presentation, it's very easy to track the source either by having a dedicated registration page for each OPN partner, or by using a UTM code (Urchin

Traffic Monitor – Google it) that tells you where each registrant came from.

This information is extraordinarily valuable because you can very quickly analyze not only where your largest volume of registrants come from, but you can also track them through to the numbers of purchases and decide which source has proved to be the best quality and most profitable.

There's money in measurement.

And all of this can be set up so that it is systematic and automatic.

The same cannot be said for most forms of off-line marketing.

9. Online meetings facilitate reminders that are 100% automated

There is a lot of misinformation about the value of reminders.

You'll read alleged statistics that attempt to prove that reminders will increase attendance rates by as much as 50%.

I can't tell you that's a lie, but I can tell you that, after testing literally hundreds of events and many thousands of attendees, reminder notices only give you a small bump in attendance levels.

It's how you articulate that core value proposition (the benefit) of attending the meeting that drives higher attendance levels.

Also the time and day of the meeting is a critical determinant of attendance levels. More on that soon.

Everything else is window dressing.

Having said that, if I can get a 2% to 5% bump in my attendance rates by setting up reminders that are automated, then of course I'm going to do that.

Just don't make the mistake of believing that an automated reminder system can compensate for a week value proposition.

It never has and never will.

10. With online meetings you can automate 100% of your follow-up

Depending on the call to Action (see next chapter), anywhere between 50% and 70% of new client inquiries or purchases comes from the follow-up sequence, which we run over the four consecutive days that immediately follow my online presentation.

My follow-up sequence is highly sophisticated and includes a 22 page PDF summary of my presentation, a five-minute "whiteboard video" summary of my presentation, a one-page PDF blueprint model that also summarizes my presentation together with simple email reminders, landing pages, and other fancy pants hard-to-set-up assets.

(If you register and attend my online presentation, then you'll receive copies of all of these Assets as a part of my follow up. Just go to www.LeadGenDemo.com and register there.)

But frankly, the very simple email reminder follow-up sequence that I developed prior to the more sophisticated sequence I've just mentioned, worked almost as well.

The conclusion for this section is therefore that it's not so important *how* you follow-up, but rather that you *do* follow-up over the days that follow your presentation, because you'll generate a very significant number of additional inquiries and sales by doing so.

People who don't follow-up their presentations with a repetition of their offer are leaving an enormous amount of money on the table and are failing to maximize the return on the time and effort that they invested in getting their Audiences to attend and in actually making their presentation.

And with online meetings, the massive extra increase in inquiries and sales can be set up as an online system so that that extra profit is 100% automated.

How to Immediately Establish Your Brand as Different and Trustworthy

There are so many people who appear to be successful through hyping up their marketing and making exaggerated promises and claims that the words "hype" and "success" could be mistaken for being synonymous.

It is unfortunately true that there are a lot of people out there that BS and hype their way to flogging products and services, which are not what they make them out to be.

The common tactic with some of these marketers is what is referred to as "bait and switch."

That means that what you think you are getting is not what you're going to get.

For example, let's say that you see a Facebook advertisement which offers you a free bottle of high-quality aromatherapy oil.

You click on the link and arrive on a slick sales page which includes testimonials and claims of miraculous healing powers possessed by this free bottle of oil.

You then click through to another web page which asks you a series of "qualifying" questions and to your delight it appears that you are one of the very few who qualify.

You click through to the order page where you suddenly find that you'll receive your "free" bottle of miraculous healing oil when you order five bottles for only $97.

That's classic bait and switch.

And you've probably experienced something similar when you've attended a webinar.

The webinar is promoted as a "free training" and indeed it may have included some valuable ideas, but the last 20 minutes was a fever-pitched offer from the presenter to buy something that's heavily discounted, complete with bonuses valued at a small fortune, all yours provided you buy before the flashing countdown timer hits zero.

That's not the worst example of bait-and-switch I can think of, but it's still misleading marketing.

You were offered a free training that was promoted as being valuable. No mention was made that there was going to be a sales pitch.

And it's most likely that the presenter told you what you needed to do in order to realize the benefit promoted, but not how to do it.

That's an old marketing presentation trick: tell what to do but not how to do it. Another variation of bait-and-switch.

Personally, I don't have a big problem with someone offering a free training and including a call to action at the end, so long as the latter is simple and straightforward and not hyped up and they don't engage is artificial scarcity created through the use of some BS countdown timer which miraculously resets itself every 24 hours anyhow.

But I do have a *bit* of a problem with it.

And the wee small problem I have is this: if your very first experience of my brand is one where I am less than fully transparent and honest about what your experience will be, why should you then trust me to be any more transparent and any more honest *after* you've paid me money and become a client?

I remember in 2016 the great debate was whether presidential nominee Donald Trump would change his behavior and become more presidential-like if he was elected president.

I clearly recall many commentators suggesting that he would cease with the personal insults and other symptoms of narcissistic behavior once he became president.

Guess what?

He didn't.

And neither should we have expected him to.

For all his faults, Donald Trump, does not practice bait-and-switch.

For better or worse, with Donald Trump, what you see is what you get.

And so it should also be with you and with me: we should promote our online presentations as a demonstration of how we work with our clients and how they realize the benefits that they were seeking when they signed up with us.

That's why I don't recommend promoting your online presentation as a free training webinar, if it's going to include something else.

A common comment that I receive from new clients is that they were impressed by my authenticity and honesty.

They report that they found my more direct approach was refreshing and gave them some confidence that once they became a client, they would continue to experience the same theme of openness, directness, authenticity and transparency.

By promoting your online presentation as a demonstration of how you work with your clients, you'll immediately be seen as more honest and more authentic and more trustworthy than the majority of your competitors who position their webinars as a "free training."

HOW TO INCREASE CONVERSIONS FOR HIGH-TICKET SERVICES, AND FOR SENIOR EXECUTIVE PROSPECTS

I mentioned above about the myth that busy senior executives will not attend a webinar.

In part, that's true.

They won't attend a webinar if they think that their experience will be less then relevant, pertinent and a valuable use of the time relative to other options.

If a senior executive is in enough pain career-wise, or if they sense a big enough opportunity, they will register for and they will attend your online presentation.

It's as simple as that: people will be motivated by the avoidance of pain or the by the pursuit of potential provided they feel either of those twin motivators powerfully enough.

But there is a little twist that I can add to the idea of marketing to busy executives, or prospects for high-ticket services via an online presentation that will increase your registration and attendance numbers.

When you promote your online presentations webinar, there is an assumption by your prospects that your attendance is going to be somewhat anonymous.

The assumption is that they will be one of dozens or hundreds or thousands of people and that they will simply be listening in to what you have to say.

And most likely they will also assume that if your presentation is not interesting or valuable that they'll be able to clear the emails, check their Facebook feed and finish the tax return, while you drone on.

In other words, their assumption that they will be an anonymous "one of many" lowers their level of commitment and engagement and thereby lowers the perception of the likely value they will receive in exchange for attending your presentation.

But that all changes when you reposition your online presentation from a webinar to a "Boardroom Briefing" with a limit of eight attendees and with webcams on.

Gone is the idea of a large crowd of attendees.

Gone is the idea of anonymity.

Also gone is the idea of lower levels of engagement and a complete lack of personalization and customization.

The idea behind a Boardroom Briefing is that you sacrifice the potential for a larger audience and cater for lower numbers but with higher levels of engagement and commitment and conversions from attendees to clients.

Our conversion rate for Boardroom Briefings is three times that of our larger webinar type online presentation.

That means that I'll only run a Boardroom Briefing when I'm targeting senior executives or when I'm targeting a segment that's prepared to pay for a high-ticket price service such as a done-for-you lead generation system that's implemented into their business.

So if your target market falls into either of those two aforementioned categories, then consider promoting your online presentations as Boardroom Briefings and not as webinars.

And in your promotion, make it explicit that you are limiting the meeting to 8 attendees and that it will be webcams on.

THE EIGHT OBJECTIVES TO ACHIEVE WHEN RUNNING ONLINE PRESENTATIONS

Presenting an online meeting for marketing purposes requires a very different method of presenting a training meeting.

It's not enough to simply present a series of slides about your service.

That's bordering on Hugh Jackman Marketing.

There is a lot to achieve in your presentation, before you even begin talking about how you work with your clients.

To be more specific, your online presentation needs to achieve eight very specific objectives which are as follows:

1. A **Demonstration** of your capability of delivering on the promise you've made in your title.

2. That your service possesses **Differentiation** – that what you have is unique and proprietary.

3. The rational, logical and ethical **Elimination** of what your audience perceives are their other options.

4. Your audience feels a sense of **Identification** – that you know where they are at and where they want to get to, as well as knowing their experiences and the frustrations that they have endured on their journey while trying to achieve what you can help them with.

5. The **Education** of your audience so they understand how you work with your clients and what the core features and benefits of your service are.

6. **Qualification** of Audience members so they know who you work with and who you can't work with and whether they fit your ideal client profile.

7. The **Eradication** of obstacles in the mind of your ideal client including financial risk, emotional risk, and the risk of wasted time, that unless eliminated would prevent them from reaching out to you.

8. The **Motivation** of those attendees who are your Ideal Clients, so they feel compelled to respond to your call to Action.

If you contrast those eight marketing-based objectives with the relatively simple objective of imparting knowledge during a training presentation, then I'm confident you'll immediately realize that the content and sequence of your online presentation is going to have to be carefully put together, in order for it to generate new client inquiries from it.

THE PERSUASION SEQUENCE: AN ITEM-BY-ITEM AGENDA EXAMPLE OF HOW TO RUN ONLINE PRESENTATIONS

As mentioned above, both the sequence and content of your presentation must be put together in such a way so that the eight objectives outlined above are achieved.

Here's my classic "Persuasion Sequence" agenda, described item-by-item, that facilitates the achievement of those eight objectives.

Your title slide

This is where you present your core value proposition.

The title must contain the explicit benefit of attending your online presentation and it must present that benefit in a manner that is differentiated so that it gets the attention of your ideal client.

A case in point is the title of my current presentation which is as follows:

DEMONSTRATION

How Professional Clients in

27 Cities and 15 Time Zones Around the World Are

Generating A Weekly Flow of Inbound, New Client Inquiries

(and without significant cost or complication)

45 minutes + Q&A

A lot of people make the mistake of thinking that the title of your online presentation needs to be the same as your unique sales proposition (USP) or elevator pitch.

But the reality is that, with the title for a presentation, you get a lot more real estate to play with than you do with either a USP or an elevator pitch.

And if you can use those extra words to increase the powerful articulation of your benefit, then use it you should.

I could have a title slide that simply said: "A New Lead Generation Method For Professionals" and that would be accurate, but it would not get the cut-through that I achieved by articulating the benefit of attending in clearer and more specific terms.

One of my best tips for creating a title that gets cut-through and increases desire is to include specificity.

When you do it right, specificity increases desirability and believability.

For example, you'll notice that in my title I've included the fact that I have clients in 27 cities and 15 time zones around the world.

That sort of specificity greatly enhances the perception of differentiation and that in turn get you more cut-through (more attention) than by simply writing about lead generation in a more general way.

Also note that I've included the anticipated duration of the presentation and the fact that there will be a question-and-answer session. These are not essential elements, but they help increase certainty for the registrant in terms of their commitment (the duration) and enhances their perceived benefit (the Q&A).

In summary, make sure that your title sounds different from whatever your competitors are offering.

And make sure that the benefit of attending is explicit.

Finally, position your presentation as a demonstration and not a free training webinar so you show transparency and directness, right from the get-go.

Agenda item 1: Who will benefit

Each agenda item introduces the purpose of each part of your presentation.

And often each agenda item is an opportunity for you to repeat the promise that's embedded in the title of your presentation.

Having said that, the specific reason for agenda item number one is to give people confidence that they are in the right place and that they are going to obtain the value they are looking for.

I only use one slide to achieve this and that one slide states the following:

Who Will Benefit

Professionals offering advice, service or software where the average sale is thousands of dollars.

Who want to enjoy a predictable weekly flow of high-quality, inbound, new client inquiries.

With that one slide I have identified my ideal client and assured those attendees who fit that description that they are in the right place and that I'm going to cover the content that they are seeking.

That slide also gives me the opportunity to repeat the benefit of working with me and ramps up my attendees' motivation levels just a bit more.

Agenda item 2: Why Listen To Me?

Because the terms "marketing" and "BS" are practically synonymous in the minds of many of my attendees, it's incumbent upon me to state in clear and specific terms why I'm different from the BS artists that they might have had the misfortune of experiencing in the past.

And I mean, isn't it a great question? Why *should* people listen to me?

Frankly, unless I can answer that question in a manner which is both clear and convincing then I don't deserve to occupy an hour of my attendees' time.

"Why Listen To Me?" consists of four slides in my presentation.

The first slide has a photo of me and images of the books that I've written.

Most of my clients haven't written books, so they replace those images with their logo or anything else that's graphically relevant and impressive.

When I click and reveal that slide, I talk for no more than 30 seconds and I only mention my experience that is relevant experience to lead generation.

I don't include any other successful experience or any other type of positive results that I have helped clients achieve in almost four decades, other than what is relevant to the subject of lead generation.

And in almost 40 years of sales and marketing, I also developed expertise in disciplines such as human resources, strategic planning, project management and a host of other leadership and management skills.

But none of them are mentioned other than those that are related to my marketing capability.

So don't bore your attendees with where you graduated from unless you need to reinforce the fact that you have academic qualifications that support the idea that you know what you're talking about when it comes to delivering the promise that's embedded in your title slide.

Storytelling is one of the latest and greatest trends in marketing.

I haven't jumped on board that bandwagon very often, however I believe that story telling is a terrific way to establish relatability with an audience and to reinforce your capability of delivering on the promise that's in your title.

With storytelling, you can talk about where you *were* at (where your Audience is probably at) and where you are *now* at (where your Audience wants to get to).

"I was fat and/or unhealthy and now I am slim and/or healthy."

"I was broke and now I am wealthy."

"My teams were underperforming and now they are overperforming."

Storytelling is particularly relevant if you're launching a new business and you don't have a bunch of powerfully explicit benefit-rich testimonials that you can reveal on the other three slides that are a part of the agenda item "Why Listen To Me?"

But because I have a lot of successful clients who have volunteered benefit-rich testimonials, I use those instead of telling my story about how I searched the world for effective inbound lead generation methods but came up short and how I used to be broke but how once I figured out inbound lead generation I became wealthier and more successful.

If you have explicit and benefit-rich testimonials from clients, then use them, but make them short and to the point.

Two short sentences are all you need.

For example, one of my delighted clients who targets senior executives emailed me a testimonial in the form of several paragraphs, describing his success. But I edited it dramatically and simply to show the following on his testimonial slide:

Thanks to the Leadsology® model, I now have a full pipeline of new client inquiries from Directors and C-Suite Execs of some of the world's biggest food corporations including Coca-Cola, Mars and Unilever.

Derek Roberts, Consultant, TasteEmotions™

If you don't have benefit-rich testimonials like this, then by all means tell your story of "before-I-discovered-this-method-my-life/business-sucked" and you're "after-I-discovered-this-method-my-life-is-great."

Agenda item 3: What's The Promise?

Neuro Linguistic Programming (NLP) and those that went before it, including Maxwell Maltz (*Psycho Cybernetics*), Dennis Waitley (*The Psychology of Winning*), all tell us that it's very difficult for the unconscious mind to distinguish between a thing that is vividly imagined and a thing that is real.

The opportunity with this agenda item is to paint a picture in the mind of the attendee that has them imagine the transformation they'll experience after they are finished working with you.

To be clear, this is not a matter of having them imagine being what it's like to work with you, but rather the benefit that follows from having done so.

In order to stimulate their imagination, you need to not only describe the benefit of having worked with you; you will also need to describe the sensory experience of that transformation by telling them what they will feel or see or hear or smell or taste, depending which senses are the most relevant.

Here what's on the slide that I use to bring to life the promise that I make, once a client has implemented my method:

THE PROMISE

You wake up every Monday morning and while sipping your coffee, you open your calendar and you feel a smile spread across your face as you see bookings from prospective Ideal Clients who want to know more about working with you and...

- *These bookings are inbound*
- *They know your fee range and can afford you*
- *The timing is good for them to start*
- *They know how you work and they like that*
- *They hope to confirm you have what they need*

Notice how I create a picture and the experience in their mind, of sipping their coffee.

I also invoke the physical sensation of feeling a smile spread across their face.

And I make use of their visual sense as well by having them imagine looking at their calendar.

And then I stack the benefits in a way that the most successful infomercials do, by revealing additional bullet points that each is benefit rich in its own right. It's like "but wait, there's more!"

(Yes, I hate informercials too, but there's a reason why they keep running the darned things: the formula works.)

It's important to note that every block of text on every bullet point is revealed one at a time.

You never want to present your audience with a large block of words.

Progressive reveal or the use of "animations," as they are referred to in Microsoft PowerPoint, are important so that your audience members will take in every word that you're showing them, word for word.

Agenda item 4: Where's The Proof?

It's almost inevitable that the best prospects attending your online presentation will have purchased from your competitors in the past and that they will have had a less than satisfactory experience.

That being the case, most of your best attendees are going to be skeptical.

You simply cannot expect for them to take your word for it, that you are good at what you do.

You must provide them with evidence that removes any reasonable doubt from their mind regarding the fact that you can deliver on the promise that's inherent in the title slide.

The best proof is visual and objective.

Numbers.

Metrics.

Photos.

Copies.

Inarguable facts.

For example, how much weight did your last three weight-loss clients lose on average? Can you demonstrate that with "before and after" photos?

Or show me the before and after Key Performance Indicator dashboards from your last three clients who hired you to increase the engagement and productivity levels of their team members.

In my case, I show screenshots which are copies of both our booking system showing the number of inbound, new client inquiry bookings that have been made, as well as a separate screenshot showing the volume of new sales, taken from our online shopping cart.

If you don't have objective numbers or images as proof, then use the next best thing, which is what I call the "Sam and Pam" scenario and reword the agenda item to "What's The Transformation?"

In this refinement of "The Proof," you show a picture of "Sam" who is a fictitious but typical *before* client scenario and all of his related pain and frustration. In other words. you paint the picture of your Audience members in terms of what they are currently suffering because they don't have your solution implemented into their business or life.

Then you switch to the "Pam" slide, showing an equally fictitious but also equally typical client *after* they finished working with you and you describe the opposite of the symptoms and related pain and frustration that you articulated when you are talking about Sam.

This before and after scenario, of fictitious but typical pre- and post-client examples, are not as powerful as metric, objective images, but they still work pretty darned well.

Agenda item 5: The Three Principles

In Chapter Three, I outlined the Five Key Principles that underpin effective inbound lead generation.

I wrote about avoiding Hugh Jackman marketing, that dogs should stick to barking, that water filters only work when you have both volume and filters, that your book needs a "different better" cover and that you should never outsource your oxygen supply.

In my own online demonstration, I limit these Key Principles to just three because I have less real estate than I have in this book.

Nevertheless, the Key Principles are a critical part of any Persuasion Sequence, be they embedded in a book or an online presentation.

What we are looking to achieve here is to create a series of "light bulb" moments where you take your Audience from not knowing a thing, to suddenly appreciating the truth of that same thing. We achieve this in a way that is analogous to having them sitting in a dark room and then turning the light on.

By creating these lightbulb moments, your credibility as the person who can lead them out of their ignorance and "darkness," and toward the promised benefit-rich land of their desires, is significantly enhanced.

In addition to that, this agenda item is designed to set up the next section which is "The Demonstration" of how you work with your clients, by highlighting the foundational principles that explain why your methodology is so effective.

In my online presentation, I precede my demonstration of the best Audience, the best Asset and the best call to Action, with the Key Principles, just as I have done in this book.

It's worth repeating that I do this so that when I cover The Demonstration (of my method) item of my agenda, my attendees' perception of the effectiveness of my method is dramatically enhanced because I'm actually bringing those Key Principles to life in the Demonstration of my methodology.

The principles are initially presented deliberately as a metaphor or an analogy and as such are designed to be cryptic and not easily understood. That's the equivalent of having my Audience sitting in the dark. When I tell them the Key Principles, they won't understand what I mean.

For example, instead of talking about "avoiding Hugh Jackman marketing," I could simply say that you need to create an opportunity for prospects to get to know you before you present them with the idea of talking about working together.

But if I explained the principle that way, there would be no lightbulb moment.

It would be simply stating what many people believe they already know, even though they may not be currently practicing it.

Your Key Principles must therefore be presented in a way that's cryptic, otherwise your attendees don't have the experience of metaphorically sitting in the dark and having you turn the light on.

It's just not as enlightening otherwise (pardon my pun).

Never underestimate the importance of preparing your attendees' minds prior to showing them your demonstration.

It takes me a solid 25 minutes to get to The Demonstration part of my agenda.

Contrast that to many presenters who fail to till the ground of their Audiences' minds before they sow their seeds.

And at the risk of plagiarizing a quite well-known spiritual teacher, the seeds that fall on the hard and closed ground of the mind, will never take root and grow.

Agenda item 6: The Demonstration

The Demonstration is the part of your presentation where you answer the question that the audience member will have in their minds in regard to your service: *"how does it all work?"*

And by the end of this section you want them to think *"Ah yes, I can see how that would work very well."*

So far, we've used your presentation to show that you are capable of delivering on the promise you've made in your title.

We've motivated the audience with your promise.

We've also provided evidence of how well your service works, and we've built a platform (The Three Key Principles), to validate the effectiveness of your methodology.

We've ethically motivated your audience members and brought them to a point where they want to know how you work with your clients.

As mentioned above (it's worth repeating), when the Audience completes The Demonstration part of your online presentation, you want them thinking *"yes, this makes sense, I can see how it would work well for me."*

A lot of marketers argue that people buy based on emotion and justify their purchase afterwards with logic.

That's only true in some situations.

If your Audience is comprised of sophisticated buyers who have a lot of experience, then they will want to justify their purchase *before* they hand over their money.

We therefore need to make sure that The Demonstration confirms that the way you work with your clients will result in the transformation that you have promised your Audience in your title slide.

And remember my maxim: *"complication destroys motivation."* Keep your explanation of how you work with your clients very simple.

Try to stick to three parts.

As a case in point, when I first launched Leadsology®, my online presentation included all ten parts of my Leadsology® Model that I wrote about in my book *Leadsology®: The Science of Being In Demand.*

I thought the 10-part model would translate well from my book into a one-hour online presentation, but I was wrong.

I didn't generate the sales that I thought I should be generating.

So, I simplified my model to just three parts: The Audience, The Asset and The Action (sound familiar?) and as soon as I did that, my sales jumped back up to where I thought they should be.

Complicated destroys motivation.

A thing needs to be as long as it takes to get the job done and then as short as possible.

The three parts I just mentioned were taken from my original 10-part model, but they in no way represent the entirety of how I work with a client.

And they don't need to do.

They only need to convince you that I can deliver on my promise of showing you how to generate a weekly flow of high-quality, inbound, new client inquiries.

Anything more is superfluous and runs the risk of confusing you and thereby lowering your motivation levels.

If, like me, you have a model that includes more than three parts, choose to either reformat it into a three-part model, as I have done, or tell your Audience that you don't have enough time to cover the whole model and that you're going to feature three parts which will provide them with the most value in the time that you have.

Then pick the three parts that do the best job of demonstrating how you bring to life The Three Key Principles in your model so that you validate how effective your method is.

You don't need to comprehensively describe your three chosen parts. Only give enough detail to answer the audience's question *"how does it all work?"* so that, by the end of your presentation, they are saying to themselves – *"yes, this makes sense, I can see how it would work well for me."*

Agenda item 7: What to Implement This?

There are two parts to this agenda item.

The first part includes a very simple slide of the key features of how you work with your clients.

In my case, that includes the fact that we have an **online program** (this is the first feature) where clients can access and implement our lead generation system (Audience, Asset and Action) at their own pace.

One the same slide, I highlight our weekly online **Implementation Support Sessions** (second feature) in the form of small group webinar meetings where my co-coach and I can help to make the implementation of the online modules faster and simpler and easier and more effective.

And on that slide, I also mention our **Client Communication Centre** (third feature) where our clients can direct-message my support team and me with questions in between the live Implementation Support Sessions.

You need to keep this part of your presentation very simple.

For me, those three features mentioned above are presented on one slide and I move through them quickly.

You don't have to go into a lot of detail.

Detail belongs on your website's sales page (e.g. www.iWant-Solo.com) which you can direct people to at the end of the webinar if you are offering for people to sign up directly to become a client, as opposed to you offering them a Consult. I'll cover both options in the next chapter.

The second part of this agenda item is your Call to Action.

What does an attendee need to do in order to take the next step toward working with you?

And that's what I'm going to be covering in the next chapter, so I won't go into any detail here.

Agenda item 8: Questions and Answers

Most of your attendees won't ask questions.

And the ones who do will typically ask a lot of questions.

It seems that these are the two types of people who attend online presentations: those who don't ask questions and those who ask a lot of questions. The latter are a small minority.

So, you'll need to moderate the Q&A to make sure that a small number of people are not hogging the time.

One way to get the ball rolling so that those people who are more reluctant to ask questions start to feel engaged, is to have two or three sample questions that you trot out at the start of the Q&A.

Typically, what I'll say something like this *"while you're thinking of questions you might like to ask, let me just give you a couple of the questions that normally come up and my responses."*

Then I can ask questions about whether there is a money-back guarantee or what level of technical expertise is required or if this works for people in retail and so on.

Note that while you are covering the Q&A, you should keep your Call To Action slide visible on the screen, which may include a link for people to reach out and book a time to talk with you (e.g. www.BookAChatWithTom.com) or it may include a link for them to go ahead and enroll in your program (e.g. www.iWantSolo.com).

Either way, keep that Call To Action slide visible during the Q&A so that people know how to take action.

How to Increase Attendance Rates

As mentioned above, you will read all sorts of ideas about how to generate a higher number of attendees relative to registrants.

Most of it is BS.

It's simply someone's guess as to what they believe should work better.

Mostly, even the confident-sounding professionals haven't tested the numbers in sufficient quantity to come up with any meaningful or reliable conclusions.

So they just spout off some confident-sounding statistics and then you and I race off and waste our time setting up all sorts of complicated SMS reminders systems only to discover that the results were almost exactly the same as before.

There are two primary factors which will determine your attendance rates.

The first is a level of motivation in your registrants.

The second is how well you articulated the benefit of those registrants attending.

It is this intersection between your ideal prospect and your value proposition that drives attendance rates up.

Everything else is either useless or of lesser importance.

Having said that, there are a few items which are worth noting and these are based on my observations from split-testing across more than 3,000 attendees.

You should note that a competent data scientist will probably quite rightly suggest that in order to arrive at conclusions that are "statistically significant," I would need to split-test two lots of 30,000 attendees.

Nevertheless, I believe that I've done enough testing to ensure that the following tips in regard to increasing attendance rates are going to of value to you.

Your promise

As stated above the biggest determining factor of attendance rates is **the promise that's embedded in your title** and how well you've articulated that promise.

Your pipeline

The second most important factor is **the source of your registrants**.

If you buy an email list and promote your online presentation to those people, then your attendance rates will be less than 5%.

If, however, you have a highly regarded industry-celebrity who has grown their email subscriber list organically via opt ins on their website and has nurtured that list with high-quality content and who has refrained from constantly pitching sales offers to that list, then your attendance rates will be closer to 40%.

On the subject of attendance percentages, they are always relative to quantity.

For example, if you run a Boardroom Briefings like I mentioned above, then you should expect 60% - 70% of the people who registered to actually turn up.

If, however, you run the more traditional, larger webinars where people expect that their lack of attendance won't be noticed, than the best you should hope for is around the 40% attendance level.

I would humbly and respectfully suggest that anyone who reports getting 80% attendance levels for a registrant list of 1,000 people is a BS artist whose hype is motivated by their goal of selling you a BS method for achieving the same fictitious result.

Your timing

The third most important factor in driving up attendance rates is **the time and day** that you conduct your online presentation.

There is no one time or day that is best for every marketplace.

If you are targeting businesses, then run your online presentation during business hours.

If you are targeting consumers who have a day job, then run them in the evenings after dinner say at 8 p.m.

If you are targeting busy executives, then don't run them on Monday mornings because they'll be in meetings.

You probably get the idea: match the time of your presentation to your market.

I've tracked the numbers for both physical seminars/workshops and webinars and found that for my target market the best time of day to run an event is 4 p.m.

That is assuming that the event will only run for one or two hours.

I've tested breakfast meetings and I've tested after-dinner meetings and I've tested lunchtime meetings and I've tested meetings that start at mid-morning and mid-afternoon.

The 4 p.m. meeting is the sweet spot for my Audience.

People can attend before they quit work, but they can still be home in time for dinner, especially if it's an online presentation.

They can get a lot of their work out of the way before attending my presentation and the team meetings are all done and now they are free to give me their undivided attention.

The best day of the week to run your meetings is either a Tuesday or Wednesday and Thursday is your next best option.

My preference is Wednesday.

The online presentations that I run at 4 p.m. Eastern USA time give me a 41% attendance rate on average.

That's 41% of the registrants actually showing up.

Outside of daylight saving, 4 p.m. Eastern USA is 6 a.m. where I live here in Australia.

I must tell you I don't much like getting up at 5 a.m. to jump in my swimming pool and then have a double espresso so that I'm awake for a 6 a.m. presentation.

So, I tested starting my online presentations at 5 p.m. Eastern USA and then 6 p.m. Eastern USA and then at 7 p.m. Eastern USA.

That meant I could sleep in a bit more.

But for every hour beyond 4 p.m. Eastern USA that I pushed my start time, my attendance percentages dropped.

I mentioned that I enjoy a 41% attendance rate when I run the meetings at 4 p.m. Eastern USA, but that drops right down to 28% when I run them at 7 p.m. Eastern USA.

That adds up to a very expensive sleep in.

Every country is a little different and every market (corporate versus small-business versus consumer) is a lot different.

The only way you can find out your sweet spot is to test and measure.

Notwithstanding that, if I were targeting business-to-business (which I am), I would start running meetings at 4 p.m. Wednesdays Eastern USA, assuming of course that I was targeting North America. If I was targeting Western and Central Europe and the United Kingdom, then I'd start the meetings at 4 p.m. Central European Time which should be 3 p.m. in the United Kingdom.

And if I was targeting consumers, I'd be starting the meetings at 8 p.m. so that families can have dinner together and so the parents get the kids to bed.

And by the way, if you think that a 41% attendance rate is not so great then you should be aware that, even with physical events, the average attendance rate that I achieved in 500 events was exactly 67%.

Furthermore, many people who regularly run online presentations are experiencing attendance rates of between 8% and 20%. So scoring 41% is actually darned good.

Your urgency

Finally, if you really want to get your attendance levels up, make sure that your email invitations are explicit that you will **not be offering a replay**. Otherwise, your attendance levels are going to be close to 12%.

BEST PLATFORMS TO RUN ONLINE PRESENTATIONS

These days there is a multiplicity of webinar platforms to choose from.

I'm big fan of GoToWebinar because it has one feature which is their "audience view window." This

feature allows me to see in real time exactly what my audience members are seeing and to synchronize my words accordingly.

You may have seen television news reporters in a foreign country who were asked a question by the newsreader. If that's the case, then you probably noticed how the reporter in the foreign country pauses for a moment before they answer that question. That's because there's a lag time when you are broadcasting from one side of the world to the other.

The GoToWebinar "audience view window" is there for a similar reason.

This feature recognizes that there is a small time delay between when I change my slide sitting here in little Castaways Beach in Queensland, Australia, and when an attendee sitting in New York or London sees that change at their end.

As mentioned, that means I can synchronize my words with what they are seeing, instead of talking ahead of what they are seeing and potentially leaving them behind.

The audience view window is *not* a critical feature and I wouldn't rush out and sign up for GoToWebinar for that feature alone. But I do like it.

The other reason that I am with GoToWebinar is that my subscription fees are the same as they were when I first signed up with them some 12 years ago.

Since then, they have significantly increased their fees, but I still get the old fees under what is known as the "grandfather clause." In other words, I've been with them so long I get the old rates.

GoToWebinar is also an incredibly reliable platform and they offer first class customer service.

Having run hundreds of webinars, I've only had two occasions where I've needed to call their customer support line, but the free calling number was answered swiftly by a human being who could immediately help me with the issue I presented. That was impressive.

Many of the less expensive webinar platforms use Google hangouts as their engine.

Have you ever tried getting customer service from Google?

They are improving but they still have a heck of a long way to go to get even close to what GoToWebinar offers.

Other than that, have a look at the webinar platform option offered by www.zoom.us which is also very stable platform.

And make sure you also check out Omar Zehhom and Nicole Balinu's www.webinarninja.com, which offers features that are truly leading edge. If I were starting out again, that's an option that I'd seriously consider.

CHAPTER SEVEN

Your Best Inbound Call to ACTION

YOUR NUMBER ONE ACTION CHOICE

IN CHAPTER FOUR, I gave you myriad options for a Call To Action but the very best one for professionals who offer services advice or software where the average transaction is in the thousands or tens of thousands of dollars is the consult.

And by "consult" I mean that meeting with a prospective client to talk with you about working together.

And true to the principle of segmentation, there are a lot of different types of consults that you can offer.

I've experimented with pretty much all of them over the last 39 years including free consults, consults that people pay for, consults that require extensive pre-meeting question-naires to be completed as well as others.

There is some merit in almost every type of consult, how-ever the very best sort are the ones that require people to move through a lot of filters before they get to speak with you one-on-one.

And for the sake of simplicity, that's the type of consult that I'll cover in this chapter.

I'll tell you when to make that offer, how to make that offer.

How to Maximize the Quality of Your Inquiries and Increase Their Motivation

One of the strange things about us human beings is that if we want a thing, then we desire it even more if we not sure if we can have it.

Marketers can ethically and rationally and logically play on this truism through a strategy that's known as "reverse psy-chology."

The idea behind this phenomenon is that people are more likely to do a thing if we tell them not to do it.

Or that they are more likely not to do a thing if we tell them that they should do it.

Either way, we ask them to do the opposite of what we want them to do.

Hence "reverse" psychology.

For example, I once bought my wife a greeting card which stated in bold type on the front of the card "do not open this card."

What would you want to do if you were the recipient of that card?

I mean aside from the fact that it's a greeting card and you'd normally open it anyway, I suspect that your curiosity would be peaked even more if you were instructed not to open it.

Or imagine that one of your preschool children had a bunch of friends over but it was raining so they couldn't play outside.

Maybe they start to drive you nuts and then the rain disappears and the sun comes out.

You could try telling them to go outside and play but chances are that they are happy where they and you wouldn't get rid of the little darlings.

But if you got their attention and collectively told them that even though the sun was out, you really want them to stay inside, you should then expect a chorus of complaints demanding that they be allowed to go outside and play.

Mission accomplished.

And it was accomplished through reverse psychology.

The type of consult that I advocate is not exactly reverse psychology in its true form but it's similar.

And it does have the advantage of increasing desirability and motivation by clearly signaling to the prospect that, despite their hopes and dreams, what I have may not be a good fit for them.

Authentically sowing that small amount of doubt in their minds is enough to increase desirability via the power of reverse psychology.

If you simply have a "book a free consult" offer on your website, then you're failing to utilize the power of reverse psychology, and even worse, it's more likely that you are stimulating a response from your prospect that's on a spectrum somewhere between apathy and aversion.

The moment that people perceive that you want to talk to them more than they need to talk to you is the moment that their motivation evaporates like a raindrop on a hot pavement.

In the previous chapter I mentioned that agenda item number seven in your presentation was "Want To Implement This?"

And that this is where you are going to place your call to Action.

At time of writing, here's what I include on that slide in my online presentations:

What you need to know to move forward:

- *Leadsology® is not a training program, it is an implementation program*

- *It takes at least 8 weeks to implement at 8 hours a week – the leads flow after that*

- *Starts @ US$XXX/month over 12 months with 12 months access and support*

- *Pay nothing for 30 days while I help you implement*

- *If for ANY reason you want to cancel, you pay nothing (no questions asked if you cancel)*

www.BookAChatWithTom.com

Naturally I reveal each bullet point one at a time and speak to each one.

Remember that this is that the end of my online presentation and that once I've covered this slide, I've achieved all eight objectives that I set out to achieve as outlined in the previous chapter.

And I've made the call to Action abundantly clear by giving them my consult booking URL and suggesting they go there and have a look at the terms and conditions on the page. Once they are satisfied that is the right thing to do for them, then they should go ahead and book a time for us to talk.

And while you might need me or one of my programs to effectively implement my Audience system and my Asset methodology, this part – the call to Action - you can implement quite effectively on your own.

Simply go to www.BookAChatWithTom.com and "swipe and deploy," as we say here in marketing land.

You'll notice on that web page there is no fancy pants sales talk.

There's no reinforcement of how great I am at what I do and there are no results-based testimonials.

It's a simple and clear articulation of what will happen when we meet and what will not happen when we meet. I've achieved everything else that I needed to achieve (the eight objectives from Chapter Six) during my online presentation. I don't need to repeat that on my consult booking page.

On that page, I also explain that our meeting won't be a sales ambush but neither will it be some sort of free ideas session, but rather a conversation between two adults to see if I've got something that's going to be a good fit for their lead generation needs.

Having explained all that, I then asked them to check four boxes to confirm that we are in agreement with the conditions for meeting.

Those four boxes look like this:

The Four Agreements

☐Yes, I understand that the primary reason for meeting with Tom will be to figure out if there is a fit between my lead gen needs and what he offers. It is therefore not a free coaching session, but neither is it some sort of sales trap.

☐I confirm that if Tom and I agree that working together is a good idea, I'm ready to start in the next few weeks *(otherwise it's best to book a chat when you are ready to start)*.

☐I am aware that Tom's programs are priced at US$795, US$1,500 and US$25,000 a month (for 12 months) and I confirm that should we agree that Leadsology® is a fit for my needs, I can afford the minimum fee of US$795 a month.

☐I confirm that I have either attended a lead gen demo webinar already and if not then I commit to reviewing Tom's ten-minute replay version of his demo before our meeting (a link to will be provided in your meeting confirmation email).

Once my attendee checks all those boxes then the link to book a time with me for a one-on-one consults becomes active.

If they fail to check all four boxes and try and book a time with me, then the webpage throws up an error message.

When you set up the same webpage for your inquiries, you will be delighted with the fact the you'll easily and naturally convert 50% to 80% of the consults you conduct into high fee-paying clients.

(The percentages vary depending on your service, your market, and your pricing.)

The reason for such a high conversion rate is simple: they are so extraordinarily well-qualified.

Despite having shown literally thousands of people the webpage I mentioned above, I suspect that I would not need all of my fingers to count the number of people who have adopted it and implemented it.

I suspect that people are worried about being so aggressive in their qualifying of their prospects.

Will you get less inquiries with my style of filtering system?

Absolutely.

Will you all but eliminate tire kickers and will you stop wasting the time of prospects who were not qualified as well as your own time?

You bet.

Remember what I said before: marketing is the simple act of finding people who are looking for your offer and placing that offer in front of them.

Anything else is selling.

If you have a bunch of people booking consults with you who really can't afford to work with you, or for whom the timing is not quite right, or for whom you're not quite the right fit, then you have to start trying to convince them that working with you is the right thing to do, even when it's probably not.

That just doesn't make sense because it simply doesn't work.

What happens when people start employing manipulative sales techniques is that square pegs get pushed into round holes.

In other words, neither you nor the client feels truly comfortable about working together and the arrangement survives for two or three months and then one of you realizes the truth, which is that you shouldn't be working together, and the arrangement collapses into a heap.

Selling is what you have to do when you're marketing sucks.

Within the pages of this book I've told you everything that you need to do to make sure that your marketing is effective. You can therefore tender your resignation to the masters of selling, for the rest of your life.

Effective marketing is authentic, genuine, transparent, honest, and it's smart.

Manipulative selling techniques are inauthentic, disingenuous, opaque and dumb.

How to Eliminate Financial Risk From Your Prospects' Mind

The biggest barrier that prevents your ideal client from moving forward is the fear that they will lose money like they have in the past when they committed to programs or advisors or coaches or software that didn't deliver on the promise that was made.

This is ubiquitous in every industry.

It's the elephant in the room.

And most people skirt around the question of trust and compensate for the high level of risk that they are asking prospects to enter into, by way of bonuses that are over-inflated in their valuation.

You've got to speak to the question of risk.

You've got to address the past experiences that are sitting in the minds of your audiences.

In part, we did that during the online presentation when we covered the agenda item "Why Listen To Me?"

And in part we covered it when we showed them testimonials from happy clients.

You might also think that it could be covered in part by offering some sort of moneyback guarantee.

But even if you do all the above, there still remains a high degree of risk in the mind of your ideal client for one simple reason: everyone else they previously gave money to covered all those bases as well.

They also had impressive bios, they had impressive testimonials, and they probably even offered a moneyback guarantee.

And yet your ideal client, sitting in your Audience during your presentation, still got burned.

And you need to know that most people don't claim a moneyback guarantee.

That's a fact that mature marketers are very well aware of. They offer guarantees knowing that most people don't like asking for their money back.

Anyhow, how can it be a guarantee when your ideal client feels absolutely no guarantee that they will get their money back, should they ask for it.

Also, think about this.

If you are looking to engage a lead generation Specialist, would you be more motivated to work with them if they asked for $10,000 upfront and offered you a moneyback guarantee or would you be more motivated if they offered to work with you for 30 days and prove that their method was effective before you paid even one cent?

My offer, which of course is the latter offer, is going to win that race every time.

Not all my clients can afford to make such an offer, which is effectively a free test drive for a 30-day period. Some of my clients need to invest a lot of money in the customization of systems or programs or platforms right at the start of a new client engagement and so they still require a deposit of some description from their new clients.

But as always, the principle here is more important than the prescription.

The principle is that you must do whatever you can to eliminate or at the very least mitigate the feeling of financial risk that will logically and reasonably exist in the mind of your ideal client, by reason of the fact that they've previously been burnt by some of your competitors.

Whatever you can do to eliminate that feeling of risk without exposing yourself to possible financial disaster, you should do.

HOW TO MITIGATE EMOTIONAL RISK FROM YOUR PROSPECTS' MIND

One of the most powerful "away from" motivators is the fear of disappointment.

Just like the psychology of reciprocity is the least spoken about and yet most powerful of all marketing motivators, the fear of disappointment is one of the least addressed and yet strongest motivators that prevent your ideal clients moving forward with your offer.

Reciprocity attracts, disappointment (or at least the fear of it) repels.

The avoidance of disappointment is a reason why many parents are constantly lowering their children's expectations, because they don't want them to experience disappointment.

Don't get your hopes up. Be prepared if it doesn't work out. And so on.

The parents that engage in this sort of anti-hope behavior are only doing so because they love their children and they want to spare them from their own personal dark and painful experiences of disappointment that they endured in the past.

Back to your audience.

Financial risk is something that they will be consciously aware of and I've outlined how you can address that above.

The fear of disappointment however is deeply subconscious but nevertheless must still be recognized as a significant obstacle that makes it difficult for them to move forward and book that consult with you.

"This sounds great but what if it doesn't work for me?"

"I've heard this sort of thing before, but it didn't work out and I felt really disappointed"

"What if this is worked for all those other people but it doesn't work for me? I feel like I was a real failure and I'd be gutted if that happened?"

These are the sort of questions that your attendees will be asking unconsciously. They may not be consciously aware of them but that doesn't mean to say that it's not critical to address them.

The best way to mitigate the fear of disappointment in the mind of your attendees is to explain to them that you've made it simple and easy and fast for them to implement and to explain why the support that you offer is excessively generous.

You have a relatively short amount of time to outline that during a presentation but a website sales page, which you can direct people to at the end of your presentation, gives you a lot more time to discuss those features in detail.

So set your prospect pathway up like this:

> **Step One**: your attendee attends your online presentation.

> **Step Two**: your attendee books a time through your consult booking page (e.g. your equivalent of **www. BookAChatWithTom.com**).

> **Step Three**: your attendee gets automatically taken to a web page that thanks them for booking the consult and ask them to check their email for the confirmation.

Step Four: while your attendee is still viewing that web page, it automatically redirects to your sales page (e.g. your equivalent of **www.iWantSolo.com**).

Step Five: on that sales page you outline in detail all the support that they'll receive during the implementation process.

In my case, I write about the multiple weekly Implementation Support Sessions and the exclusive 24/7 direct messaging Client Communication Center and how I hired professional instructional designers to make sure that my program could be implemented as simply, easily and as quickly and effectively as possible.

And I also explain how we've made the *technical* parts easier and simpler to handle and how we'll even get on a live call with them and walk through those parts step-by-step if they need that.

I also explain that I personally care so much about them implementing effectively that I'm going to give them my mobile phone number.

And I explain that when I give it to them, I can do so with confidence knowing that the level of support we offer is so world-leading and so best-in-class, that I rarely get a call or message from a client on my mobile phone.

The bottom line here is that you must demonstrate explicitly to your prospects that you've got their back when it comes to implementation; that you've made this, if not idiot proof, then childproof.

The Water Filter: How to Get the Best Quality Inquiries in Abundance

Other marketers routinely profess to surprise when I explain to them that I refuse to take any money upfront for my Leadsology® Program clients and that, despite this, I give every client full and complete access to every single module that outlines how to implement my Audience, Assets and Action system.

That's right: I take no money and I hold nothing back and I provide full implementation support.

Do I get ripped off?

Yes.

But the extra clients that I pick up because of my "you don't have to trust me, take it for a 30-day free test drive" offer more than makes up for the very small minority who overtly and deliberately steal my intellectual property.

In three years of making this offer, I've only had three people who I could categorically say have deliberately ripped me off by enrolling in the program, downloading everything, and then immediately cancelling their subscription.

But aside from that very small percentage, 5% of new clients opt out before their 30-day trial expires.

In most cases, they have put in a fair effort during their test drive but for whatever reason, maybe due to sickness or the death of a loved one, they decided to opt out.

And that's okay. I made the offer and they accepted it. That was the deal. No questions asked.

The surprise expressed by my marketing colleagues at my 30-day free test drive offer is because they assume that most people can't be trusted.

And the opposite is actually true.

It's understandable that we may develop a mistrust of people given our exposure to the daily bad news stories of murders, massacres, rapes, narcissistic political leaders and other similar content that we consume via television or livestreaming, dished up to us by media services who know that they'll sell more of the product if they feature such stories.

In my experience, most people are trustworthy, but we need to consider reliability.

But they are not the same thing.

A person can be *trusted* regarding their intention to pay you, but may prove to be *unreliable* if they are not a good manager of their money.

My guess is that 99% of my new clients can be trusted in regard to integrity and that somewhere in excess of two thirds can be trusted in regard to reliability.

That reliability percentage may not be as high as I prefer but it still represents a significant majority.

But putting those two observations aside for one moment (my experience that most people are trustworthy and reliable), let's look at why my methodology stimulates such enhanced levels of trust and reliability amongst my clients.

Almost every new client of mine has been through nine filters:

- The first filter was when they subscribed to my OPN partner's email list registering their interest in growing their business or professional practice.

- The second filter was that they stayed subscribed long enough to receive an invitation via email from my OPN partner recommending that they attend my online presentation.

- The third filter was that they registered for my online presentation.

- The fourth filter was they showed up to my online presentation.

- The fifth filter was that they stayed to the end of my online presentation where they were able to hear my offer and call to Action in the form of meeting for a consult.

- The sixth filter was they went to my consult booking page, read the terms and conditions, checked all the boxes and proceeded to book a time for their consult.

- The seventh filter was later they showed up for the consult.

- The eighth filter was that we agreed it was a good idea to work together.

- The ninth filter was that separate from that meeting and without me being present, they went ahead and enrolled in one of my programs, agreeing to the terms and conditions.

It's important to note that at almost every filter, some people are filtered out.

And you *want* them to be filtered out.

Because you don't want to be talking one-on-one with people who are not qualified or not motivated or not educated about how you work with your clients.

And you don't want people signing up to be a client unless they are in total agreement with your terms for working together.

So never be disappointed when you lose numbers at any particular filter.

That's the whole purpose of the filter: to only let the right people through.

It's just like the water filter principle from Chapter Three.

You need volume *and* you need filters.

The fact is that by the time someone meets with me for a one-on-one consult, they're hoping to confirm that working with me is the right thing to do.

They are typically highly desirous of the idea of working together either through one of my programs or as a private client.

Because of this, the focus of our time together during the consult is on confirming as opposed to convincing.

Selling is convincing, marketing is confirming.

Selling feels stressful, marketing feels natural.

Because when you get your marketing right, everything about working with you just makes sense to your ideal client.

In short, you want marketing, not selling.

Once you have it set up, marketing is easier and simpler and more effective, and you'll sleep better at night.

When to Offer a Consult Versus When to Sell at the End of Your Online Presentation

One of the ideas that's mistakenly adopted by many presenters is assuming that they need to ask attendees to pull out their credit card and buy at the end of the online presentation.

There's a time and place for that, but it's not when you're starting to market high-ticket-priced services such as advice or software through the medium of an online presentation.

My recommendation is that, if you fit the above description of someone marketing a relatively high ticket-priced service, advice or software or planning or whatever through an online presentation, you start by offering the consult as described above and that when your calendar capacity is used up then, and only then, start to trial-sell at the end of your online presentation.

Last year, I shut my door for new client consults for exactly six months.

I was very concerned about servicing the existing clients that I'd taken on and honoring the deep sense of responsibility I felt in making sure that they were implementing effectively with my guidance.

I needed the five hours and more that I was spending every week on new client consults to be freed up so I could utilize them for working with my clients.

So, I shut my door for new client consults.

But I must tell you as a full-time professional marketer of close on 40 years that did not sit well with me.

Professional marketers (and professional salespeople are the same), do not rest easily and neither do they feel comfortable unless they are converting prospects and clients.

It's what we get off on.

It's like water for a fish.

We just have to have those new clients flowing in, otherwise we don't sleep well at night.

Call me an addict or call me a marketing-alcoholic, I don't really mind. But I need new client flows like I need blood flowing through my veins.

So before the start of those six months, I sat at my desk twiddling my thumbs and doodling on my yellow legal pad trying to figure out how the heck I could free up the time I was spending on new client consults but still have new clients flowing in.

It wasn't that I didn't have capacity to serve new clients, but rather I didn't have the capacity to do that while also having the capacity for investing time with the consults.

To cut a long story short, I created an offer where people could go ahead and enroll in one of my programs directly from my online presentation as opposed to going through a consult.

I still ran my online presentations with my OPN partners and with selected LinkedIn connection invitees, but instead of offering the consult at the end of the online presentation, I invited people to go ahead and enroll directly in my program.

And I did that for six months.

So, I ended up with enough people who went through both the consult call to Action offer as well as the newer "go ahead and buy now" call to Action offer.

The results were interesting.

First of all, I was delighted that my presentation converted a lot of people directly from my online presentation without going through a consult.

That was testament to two things: the quality of my OPN partners in terms of the esteem with which their email subscribers held them, and the quality of my presentation.

(Sorry, I know that sounds immodest but if my presentation sucked, I would not have enrolled so many new clients.)

Secondly, having done the math on both sides of the split test (consult versus direct offer) it was clear that I would generate almost double the revenue from the consults method versus the direct offer method.

In part, that was due to what I call the "multi-directional consult" method whereby I could direct certain prospects into higher-priced programs when they needed it and could afford it.

And where appropriate, I was also able to direct a few select individuals into an even higher-priced but more relevant "done-for-you" service.

The bottom line with your call to Action is that you should always start out offering a consult but make sure that you have both enough volume via your OPN partners as well as enough filters (see above).

That way you will maximize the return on the time investment you make when conducting those one-on-one consults.

CHAPTER EIGHT

What to Do With the 59% Who Never Show Up to Your Online Presentation

THE INDESTRUCTIBLE GROWTH of your business is assured if you will commit to 3 weekly activities:

1. Every week you do something to build your email subscriber list.

2. Every week you add value to your email subscriber list with something that's free.

3. Every week, on average, you offer a carefully sourced Audience the opportunity to book a consult with you or you invite them to go ahead and buy from you directly.

The above is what I call the Titanium Triangle and I go into more detail in my previous book *Leadsology®: Marketing The Invisible*.

I use the word "titanium" because it's stronger than steel and more valuable than gold and I use the word "triangle" because, as you can see from the above, there are three parts to the model.

The Titanium Triangle model is the perfect segue from the online presentation model that I covered in Chapters Five, Six and Seven and into this chapter on what to do after you have delivered your call to Action to your Audience via your Asset.

Once you implement my Audience Asset and Action model, you'll enjoy a regular increase in the number of email subscribers, and your email database will become the most valuable asset in your entire business.

But as you are growing that email list by way of registrants to your online presentations, you will doubtless want to maximize the opportunity to serve the 59% of registrants who fail to show up to your webinar.

And the beautiful thing about the Western capitalistic model, for all its faults, is that the more effectively you serve people the more money you make.

And that's why this chapter will show you what to do with the 59% who you could not serve because they didn't show up to your presentation.

But first, let me introduce you to my SEW Segmentation Model, because once you understand the difference in motivations of the three main categories of email subscribers, then you will understand the principles behind the creation of different types of Educational Marketing Assets (EMAs) as I've referred to general marketing Assets in my earlier books.

An EMA is simply some form of content which adds value to your email subscribers by educating them via some form of valuable content for which they will generally exchange their email address.

That however is not the context for this chapter.

Most people offer an EMA on the website.

The idea is that people visiting your website to check you out will subscribe if they are presented with an offer that is attractive enough, such as a free e-book or a free video series or whatever.

The problem with that idea is that most people have very little traffic coming to the website.

So even if you create a seriously valuable EMA (and I'll share with you the most powerful ones below), it will end up being like the neon-sign billboard stuck in the middle of the Sahara desert that I mentioned earlier in this book.

It might look amazing, but no one gets to see it.

Therefore, the idea of investing time and money and effort to create an EMA to put on your website is mostly going to give you a big fat nothing in return.

As mentioned earlier, by all means have at least one EMA on your website.

But instead of thinking that's the best way to use your EMA, let's focus on a more profitable use which is to use your EMA to target the 59% of registrants for your online presentation who didn't attend.

You may think that the lack of attendance signals a lack of interest, but I can assure you that is not always the case.

Your non-attending registrants are an absolute gold mine when it comes to generating future new client inquiries.

I am always shocked to hear of people who run webinars and either fail to have any follow-up system or worse still, fail to have every single registrant imported into their online email database for nurturing and keeping the brand in the brain until they are ready to buy.

And in case you're concerned about falling foul of anti-spam legislation, let me assure you that, if someone has registered to attend your online meeting, you are well within your spam-free rights to have that person added to your email list. Certainly, that's the case in Australia and the USA at time of writing. Of course, always check your local anti-spam regulations.

In my business, our registrants are automatically added to our email subscriber list.

That way, we can not only send them automated reminders, but we can also send them the automated follow-ups after each online presentation.

Before I dive into specifics, let's briefly review my SEW Segmentation Formula so that you understand which EMA works best for each email subscriber segment.

How to Get Five Times Your Conversions with the SEW Segmentation Formula

Not all email subscribers are the same.

I mentioned previously in this book that the concept of segmentation allows you to be more specific in meeting the needs of your prospects as well as giving you the opportunity for scalability.

Based on many years and careful analysis of both website visitors as well as registrants to my online presentations, I've been able to identify three segments within my Audiences.

The three segments I call, the Seekers, the Explorers and the Wanderers, hence the "SEW" Segmentation Formula.

3% of your audience are Seekers

Seekers are fast decision-makers and when they're see what they've been looking for they act immediately.

I am a seeker.

I see it, I want it, I buy it.

(And yes, it's a great recipe for going broke which is why I now work with a Chief Financial Officer.)

Once you've established that you've got what a Seeker wants, all you need to give them is your call to Action that shows them how to book a consult with you, or how go ahead and buy your program or service.

What's not to love about Seekers?

Not much really.

They practically sell themselves so long as you don't frustrate them by taking too long telling them how to take Action.

Just give them your sales page or shopping cart link or consult booking link.

Seekers take action and they take action fast.

The only thing I don't like about Seekers is that there are not enough of them.

Hence, 3% is not a lot unless you've got high volume but fortunately that's what my OPN and LinkedIn methods (see Chapter Five) give you.

12% of your audience are Explorers

Most of your new clients are going to be more conservative in their decision-making process than the Seekers.

Explorers represent 12% of your audience and before they buy from you, you must satisfy their need for exploration.

If you don't satisfy an Explorer's need for exploration, they'll get it satisfied by exploring your competitors' offerings.

And I can confidently tell you that this is how an Explorer behaves because we track what they do on our website.

An Explorer needs an average of five EMA exposures before they'll buy. That's a lot! The more EMAs you can offer them, the more Explorers you'll convert into Seekers who will then convert into clients.

For example, a typical new client who comes from the Explorer segment will behave something like this:

1. They receive an email invitation to attend my online demonstration from one of my OPN partners and they click on the link and register for the webinar. Whether or not they attend is a moot point at this stage.

2. If they attend the online presentation, then that's really their first added-value exposure to my brand. If they don't attend, then they will still receive the follow-up series of EMAs that we send out via email over the four days following my live presentation. So, depending on whether they attend my presentation and whether they open any of the follow-up emails, they may have experienced anywhere between one and five exposures to my brand at this point.

3. Some will attend my online presentation and go ahead and book a consult. Most of those who attend will not book a consult at this point.

4. In the meantime, whether or not they have booked the consult, they will probably check out my LinkedIn profile (**www.linkedin.com/in/tompoland/**) which includes links to my website and another EMA **www. FiveHourChallenge.com,** so that's potentially another one or two exposures to my brand.

5. The other main place that registrants go to check me out is my website at **www.Leadsology.guru** where they'll have the opportunity to opt in to any number of other EMAs including e-books, a diagnostic lead generation tool, my podcast, my Facebook group, downloading my interactive PDF lead generation guide, and a lot more.

As mentioned, Explorers buy from me after an average of five quality exposures to my brand.

They are more conservative than Seekers and that's not necessarily because their budget is tighter. It's more of a mindset thing than it is a money thing.

The bottom line with the Explorer is that if you only have one EMA, be that a webinar or an e-book or whatever, then you will fail to satisfy their need for exploration through five validations of your brand, and that means that instead of converting 15% of your Audience to clients you'll only be converting 3%.

That, on its own, may explain why you are currently short of new client inquiries.

You therefore want to start developing EMAs just as soon as you've created your online presentation.

That's the order of priority: create your online presentation first because it's the Asset/EMA that's going to build your email list with high-quality subscribers the fastest and it's the asset that is going to quickly generate that flow of high-quality, inbound, new client inquiries.

But just as soon as you have that up and running, start scrambling and develop some more EMAs.

I'll go into more detail of what I recommend for each segment below once we've dealt with the Wanderers.

85% of your audience are Wanderers

The Wanderers have no serious intent to buy anything from you. They are just wandering around the internet looking for stuff that might be interesting or valuable.

Wanderers are merely flirting with the idea of doing something with you. They have no intention whatsoever of jumping into bed with you, commercially speaking.

But please note that Wanderers are anything but a waste of your time.

They are simply not ready to buy right now.

And if they didn't have at least a modicum of intent to seek a solution, which your service can provide, they would not be wasting their time wandering around the internet looking for ideas.

With Wanderers, the key issue is not so much serving them with any particular EMA but rather simply keeping your brand in their brain until they are ready to buy.

That said, they will be more interested in an EMA that they can quickly scan as opposed to one that involves a serious investment of their time.

Simple downloadable one-page interactive models or blueprints or cheat sheets or checklists are the ideal type of EMA to offer to the Wanderers.

Your Objective With Each Segment

Imagine that it's Sunday morning and you decide to go for a walk in a forest.

You have no particular intent other than to enjoy the fresh air and beauty of a forest environment.

You leave your car and start to walk down a clear path through the forest when out of the corner of your eye you notice something well off the trail, sparkling in reflected sunlight.

Curious, you stop walking and look far into the forest where you can see the bright shimmering light.

You walk off the forest path and through the trees to the source of the sparkle and to your surprise and delight, you see that there is a large diamond lying on the forest floor, reflecting the sunlight.

You pick up the diamond and examine it and then place it carefully in the backpack you brought with you.

Question: what's the first thing you do while you're still standing there, having put the diamond in your backpack?

Answer: before you even take another step, you look around to see if there's any more diamonds.

And now you've gone from being a Wanderer to an Explorer.

And that's exactly what a great EMAs are designed to do: to convert Wanderers to Explorers and to convert Explorers to Seekers and to convert Seekers to clients.

My Top Eight Assets for Satisfying Every Prospect Segment

Here's a list of my most profitable EMAs including where possible the Conversion Rate (CR) from visitor to email subscriber, and the link to the relevant EMA.

Alongside each EMA listed below is the letter denoting the segment that is most motivated by that Asset. "S" is for Seekers, "E" is for Explorers and "W" denotes Wanderers.

Website (SEW)

URL: www.leadsology.guru

CR: 5%

Sales Page (S)

URL: www.iWantSolo.com

CR: 3%

E-Book (E)

URL: https://tompoland.lpages.co/free-leadsology-book-infusionsoft/

CR: 70%

Diagnostic (E)

URL: www.leadsology.guru/diagnostic/

CR: 47%

Interactive Model (W)

URL: www.leadsology.guru/the-model/

CR: 31%

Five Day Challenge (E)

URL: www.fivehourchallenge.com

CR: 38%

Consult Booking Page (S)

URL: **www.bookachatwithtom.com**

CR: 7%

Giveaways of High-value Programs*

ULR: Various but only offered in exclusive and limited give-aways.

CR: 81% - 97% depending on the product and OPN Partner source

* These are programs that have previously sold for hundreds of dollars in physical form (typically DVDs and workbooks) that are now offered to OPN Partners' email subscribers if the OPN Partner is not currently promoting webinars e.g. **https://www.leadsology.guru/shop/killer-referral-machine/** in which case I use a "two-step" sequence of obtaining the subscribers email address and *then* inviting them to attend my online demonstration.

CHAPTER NINE

Why You Need Me or My Program to Put All of This Into Place

A COMMON QUESTION THAT I get asked by my clients is how much of their intellectual property they should reveal during an online presentation. Their question comes from a concern about revealing too much of their "real oil."

It's quite understandable that you may also share a similar concern, which is that if you reveal too much then your prospects might mistakenly believe that can implement your ideas on their own.

In years past, I shared that concern and I followed the mantra of many marketers who say your book or seminar or webinar (or whatever EMA you are using to generate email subscribers and inquiries) should tell people *what* they need to do but to also be explicit in communicating that they will need you to show them *how* to do it.

My conclusion after all these decades in marketing is that such an approach is only partly valid.

The fact is that, as stated right at the outset of this book, what you have just read is not an implementation program and that a book simply doesn't have the capacity to walk you through the intricacies of implementing such a method.

But back to the question of how much of your intellectual property you should disclose.

Let me ask you this: is your ideal client a smart person with the money to pay for your services?

Of course, the answer is going to be a resounding "yes" and "yes."

That's because you don't want to work with people who don't have the intelligence to follow your recommendations and because there is no point in you trying to work with people who can't afford you.

Therefore, it's axiomatic and inescapable that your ideal client will possess those two characteristics: they will be smart people who have enough money to work with you.

That being the case, let me assure you that if someone is smart and they have the money, they will not be tempted, for more than a fleeting moment, to attempt to implement on their own.

They will want to pay you money because they will want your help in implementing your methods and systems and processes and models, in whatever form they come, into their business or their life.

If they are stupid, they will try to implement on their own. And I think we agree that you don't want to work with stupid people anyway.

(Remember: you can help ignorant, but you can't help stupid.)

And if they can't afford you, then you are better to give them a free EMA to help them until they can afford you.

Therefore, my recommendation is that you create your presentation to cater for the people who are smart who also have the money to pay for your services and don't be concerned about giving too much away.

As mentioned, the smart ones who have the money will want to invest in working with you because they are smart enough to realize that that is how they are going to actually get your intellectual property implemented effectively and thereby enjoy the benefits of bringing your recommendations to life.

Just be sure that you are explicit and direct in communicating the fact that they will need you to help them implement.

In just the same way as I am doing here.

If you read this far, then there is a very high probability that you're both smart and that you have the budget to pay for me or one of my programs.

That's great news for both of us.

To that end, feel free to go and signup for my SOLO program at **www.iWantSolo.com**, or if I have availability and you want to chat, you'll find a time here: **www.Book-AChatWithTom.com**.

And thanks for investing in this book.

CHAPTER TEN

Leadsology® Results

THE FOLLOWING ARE comments from clients who have graduated from one of Tom Poland's programs, which are embedded with the principles, strategies, and structure of Leadsology.® These results are from clients who "imperfectly persisted" in implementing the strategies from his program. Results like these are not achieved by all clients and results are dependent on many factors external to Tom Poland's control.

My market is CEOs and VPs of global food corporations. In the past, getting my message noticed by such senior people was difficult in the extreme.

But thanks to Leadsology® LeadStreams®, I now have a full pipeline of new client inquiries from Directors and C-Suite Execs of some of the world's biggest food corporations including Coke, Mars, and Unilever. To be honest, I'd never have thought this sort of result was possible and I'm relieved and delighted.

Derek Roberts, Consultant

Prior to Leadsology® I was generating six figures, but almost killing myself scrambling around for clients.

I'm now having more fun, generating five times the number of new clients and in less time than I ever thought possible.

Christina Force, Coach and Trainer

When we started working with Tom Poland we already had one or two marketing systems in place, but we weren't getting any results.

Then we applied the Leadsology® LeadStreams® methodology and whereas before we had frequent gaps in our bookings, now we're often booked out weeks ahead.

Gordon Dickson. Kinesiologist

During the first twelve months that I worked with Tom Poland our **revenue increased by 43% to over $1,000,000 and my net personal earning's rose by 50 % to $400,000.**
We achieved the goals with no sacrifice of personal leisure time and we continue to enjoy an "earnings per partner hour" which is amongst the top quartile in the country.

Steve Bennet, Bennet and Associates

Before working with Tom Poland's program I was very clear about where I want to take the business to, but I had no idea of how to get there and I thought, "If I work any harder I'll kill myself." **But while I was working with Tom our turnover exploded, we more than quadrupled our revenue and profits increased by over 300%.** *At the same time I worked a lot less. My investment with*
Tom has paid off more than tenfold. Tom's program certainly delivers on its promises.*

Ginny Scott, M.D. Capulet

In the first year of working with Tom my earnings increased by just over 100%.
One of the biggest benefits was discovering how to strengthen my ability to systematically attract very high quality new clients into my practice. In addition I was able to set realistic but challenging goals in my business and personal life to achieve a more realistic work life balance.

Greg Moyle. Managing Director, NZFP

The corporate business environment we work in is very complex. Our ideal clients are senior executive and C-level people for whom business is a matter of high stakes, and they are therefore slow to trust and very discerning when selecting new consultants. Tom Poland's Leadsology Program has enabled me to not only find the right leads, but to build a relationship of trust and rapport with them to the point where they have gone from barely knowing about us, to trusting us with their most critical M&A Acquisitions. As a result, I enjoy a lead pipeline that is continually full of high-quality, inbound, new client, inquiries.

Thomas Kessler, Consultant

Prior to joining Tom Poland's program I was working 60 − 70 hours a week and I had only one afternoon off work on the weekends. Now a typical work week for me is about three days. **Our profit has tripled and so I'm making a lot more money out of what I'm doing.**

Tom's program is priceless. I couldn't put a price on where the program has taken me from and where I am now.

Dianne Bussey, FACT Solutions Consulting

Anything that doubles your income has got to be good and that's exactly what happened while working with Tom Poland.

I gained an additional depth to my personal life and business life. I've got more leisure time, I have more holidays, and I earn more. I recommend Tom Poland to anyone in charge of a business.

Geoff Wilson, Professional Consulting Group

Before working with Tom Poland's program my business was "all me". I was working insane hours and I thought there had to be a better way.

Now I've freed up a lot of time including 12 weeks holiday a year as well as **growing the business by over 400% and adding several million dollars to turnover and the bottom line of my business.**

Fred Soar, Soar Printing

I started working with Tom Poland 18 months ago and already I've doubled my earnings

I now also enjoy three months holidays every year whereas for the last 31 years I've worked almost seven days a week.

I've experienced dramatic changes in both my business and personal life.

John Good, Good Financial Services

Before joining Tom Poland's program around 2000 I was working 60 – 70 hours a week. Once we started working together I grew my number of employees from six to over 30 and **I sold one of my businesses**

for many millions thanks in no small part to working with Tom's program.

I've spent a week with Richard Branson on his private island and dined personally with Google founder Larry Page thanks to Tom challenging me to think bigger and to follow my passion. And I'm pleased to still be working with Tom some eight years later. Joining Tom's program was certainly one of the best business decisions I've ever made.

Mark Rocket, Rocket Lab, Avatar and others

Before joining Tom Poland's program I'd reached a point where I couldn't see how I was going to grow the business more because I was drowning in detail. Now my time is freed up to think more clearly and more creatively. **We've gone from being static to buying out a competitor because we've boosted our profits significantly.**

And time off was always an issue for me but now I take at least one week off every quarter and three weeks at Christmas and I feel good about that. If you are prepared to make changes the value of Tom Poland's program is massive.

Ian Telford, Jason Products

As a result of working with Tom Poland the value of my business increased by many millions of dollars.

Before joining Tom's program I was working six and seven days a week. Now I achieve more and yet I only work four days a week.

My advice for any business owner who wants to enjoy more revenue and a better quality lifestyle, is to get on with it by joining Tom Poland's program.

Grant Faber, Superbrokers Logistics Ltd

In the last 12 months since I started working with Tom Poland my earnings have more than doubled and I'm ahead of my target again this year.

I've gone from having 4 weeks holiday per year to 13 weeks. I've quit smoking, lost 4 kilograms of weight and I'm fitter than I've ever been before.

I credit these achievements to my commitment to working with Tom Poland.

If you own a business then it's likely that working with Tom will be the best investment you'll ever make.

Warren Storm, Storm Financial, Life Brokers NZ Ltd

Prior to working with Tom Poland's program I was running a reasonably successful business but since then **sales have increased and profits have increased quite considerably.**

But the success at work has been balanced by ongoing success at home and with my health as well and that's been important to me.

Tom's programs may appear to be pricey but it's also a question of value because in my case, I've recovered the cost of his program many times over.

Alan Coop, Intercad Ltd

After joining Tom Poland's program **within nine months I've boosted profits and generated more revenue than the last three years put together.**

The actual overall improvement as a complete package in my business has been substantial and that's allowed me to become semi-retired.

Gilbert Chapman, Debt Recovery Group

Prior to working with Tom Poland I was working long and hard but the business wasn't growing and I felt frustrated about that.

Thanks to working with Tom my business rapidly increased in value and is now worth millions.

I can think of no reason why anyone who wants to add six or seven figures to their revenue would not apply to join Tom's program.

My investment has paid off a thousand fold. Tom's program worked with me and I know of others who have had a similar result.

Win Charlebois, The Diamond Shop